VERDICT

JESUS CHRIST IS WHO HE SAID HE WAS

A trial lawyer examines
the evidence and makes
a startling discovery

THOMAS T. ANDERSON

Verdict: Jesus Christ Is Who He Said He Was
By Thomas T. Anderson

FIRST EDITION
ISBN 0-9745280-8-0
Cover photo: Greg Schneider
Cover and interior design: Ron Kadrmas

Contact information:
Tom Anderson
Attorney at Law
45-926 Oasis Street
Indio, CA 92201
(760) 347-3364
e-mail address: ttapc@aol.com

Printed in the United States of America by Plus Communications, St. Louis, Missouri.

INTRODUCTION

Why Verdict?

My book, Verdict, has been distributed to over 4,000 readers. Many have asked, "Why did you write this book?" This question deserves an answer. Events that may seem insignificant to you but were pivotal to me will be discussed.

In the early 1930s, the Great Depression gripped this country by the throat. I was just four years old at the time, living in Seattle, where my father sold life insurance. At a time in our nation's history when unemployed fathers were selling pencils on street comers, most families didn't have any money left over to buy something as frivolous as life insurance, not when you had a set of hungry mouths sitting around the dinner table.

Since I was a single child, Dad had fewer mouths to feed, but that was cold comfort during a time of economic disaster. Then my father heard of an opportunity in Silverton, Oregon, so he moved the family there and plunked down his life savings to purchase Anderson Motors, a Ford dealership.

Located twelve miles northeast of Salem,the state capitol, Silverton was nestled at the foot of the Cascade Mountains and resembled a Swiss village, complete with an alpine river running through town called Silver Creek. Some ten to twelve miles away in the Cascade Mountains, Silver Creek formed ten spectacular falls, some higher than Niagara Falls. Silver Creek ran alongside my Dad's dealership, where I and my newfound friends fished from the banks. In a town of 2,000, everyone knew each other.

My mom, Gladys, was an accomplished musician who at one time had the potential for singing soprano at the Met. Growing up in a flyspeck of a town—Mayville, North Dakota—diminished her chances of performing in New York, however. She was raised in the same neighborhood—actually, across the alley—from a young man named Tom Anderson. After they married and I came along, my mother was content giving singing lessons, directing the church choir, and playing a lively piano for friends. She was vivacious, energetic, and, as far as I know, without an enemy in the world.

My dad was more subdued but certainly no shrinking violet, known for his dry sense of humor and many friends. After we set down roots in Silverton, Dad wasn't fulfilled by selling Fords and haggling with customers. I heard him say years later that he preferred the short stint he had teaching American History at a small town high school in Montana. Although life did not work out as he had hoped at the Ford dealership, Dad hung in there. I loved them both very much, and he and Mom also loved each other. They raised me in an exemplary fashion. I can't be critical of them in any way.

I have to say that growing in the rural environment of Silverton was a Tom Sawyer-like existence. To me, it was about as good as life can get. Drugs were unheard of, and nobody locked their doors. I can't recall anybody getting a divorce. The only thing I didn't like were Sunday mornings.

I remember a typical Sunday, one year before the start of World War II, when I woke up to the sound of rain pelting the shake roof of our home. It was always raining in Silverton during the winter months, but there was one thing worse than the pitter-patter of the rain—going to church with my parents. I did not look forward to Sundays. The church we attended was very boring. The parishioners seemed sullen and preferred talking about the most uninteresting subjects. Sundays were just downright unpleasant.

My worst experience at church was attending a confirmation class conducted by Pastor Fuhr, who made us memorize verses. Few questions were allowed, although one time I mustered the courage to ask him why I should believe the Bible is true. "Just fear the Lord, that is all you need to know," he replied tersely.

I thought he would give me a better answer because he was our pastor and should know about such things. Incredibly, that was his total explanation. This evasive answer confirmed my growing Christian skepticism, however, and nurtured my burgeoning unbelief. It seemed that no one in my life could or did explain the truth concerning Jesus Christ to me, including my parents. Dad and Mom never shared with me what or why they believed—or even ask me if I believed in Jesus Christ as my Savior.

Perhaps they were afraid to ask. Whatever their reason, as I came of age and settled into life as an agnostic, I concluded that their failure to talk about their Christian beliefs was because they knew nothing persuasive about the claims of Christ. That is probably why I really had nothing to do with church once I left home and was on my own.

After Dad retired at the early age of fifty, my parents moved to Pasadena, California. After another twenty years, they moved into a nursing home. Shortly thereafter, Mom died of diabetes at the age of seventy, and Dad followed her exactly six 'months to the day after Mom died, succumbing to Parkinson's disease at the age of seventy-two. When they were alive, I feigned a relationship with Christ since they were believers. I did not want to disappoint them, but I was living a lie. 1 doubt if 1 successfully fooled them, but at least I tried.

After their deaths, I was released from this bondage, which allowed me to seriously consider whether Christ was real for the first time. But before that happened, I discovered my parents' Bibles. Both Bibles were well worn and contained revealing notes confirming their faith. At that time, even though I was an agnostic, it seemed odd to me that they had not shared their faith with me. I again concluded the reason for this failure was because their faith was unsupportable.

Different Priorities

I started working on a farm two miles north of Silverton at the age of nine. I didn't need the money, however. It seemed that I had an urge to work from an early age. My friends asked why I was working because in Silverton, our family had the reputation of being rich, which by the standards of our small town, we were. This work ethic, for the first twenty years of my law practice, kept me from considering the claims of Christ. That's not where my priorities lay. My first priority was building a career as a trial lawyer, and everything else was secondary—including any consideration of the claims of Christ. This work ethic completely slammed the door on even considering if Jesus was real.

I enrolled at the University of Oregon in Eugene when I was only fifteen years old. I cannot recall anybody on the Eugene campus, teacher or student, even casually discussing religion, but then again, the U of O was a secular university. Students were more interested in Saturday night beer blasts or conducting a panty raid at the Delta Gamma house than in having Bible studies.

I belonged to a fraternity, and when my fraternity brothers heard about my plans to attend the University of Willamette Law School in Salem after graduation, they wagered whether I would last two semesters. I fooled them, as well as myself, when I performed well in law school. You could say that jurisprudence agreed with me.

After attending law school for two years at Willamette, I was encouraged by a friend to join the Oregon Air National Guard so that I could complete the third year of law school before going into the armed forces. By this time World War II had ended. I joined the Guard on a Friday and the unit was activated Saturday. Timing was everything. After attending Officer Candidate School at Lackland Air Force Base in Texas, I was assigned to the Office of Special Investigation (O.S.I.) and shipped off to Thule Air Force Base in Greenland, a mere 450 miles from the North Pole, for a one-year hitch.

At this northern outpost, both of my feet were firmly planted in the frozen tundra of agnosticism. Like many who were ambivalent about the existence of God, I took it as an article of faith that Darwin's theory of evolution was true. One clear sunny day with the temperature a frigid 50 degrees below zero, I took a leisurely walk over a field of solid ice. Suddenly, something colorful caught my eye in the sea of white: a lonely but beautiful purple,and,white flower peeking from beneath the ice. I have no idea how a fragile, one-inch tall flower could have existed in this stark, uninhabitable climate, but there it was. I was totally confounded as to how this purple-and-white flower could have evolved or even existed in such an icy environment, so I questioned Darwin's theory. This conclusion, I thought, was shameful and heretical so I wouldn't admit it to anyone.

Being isolated for a year in an area surrounded by icebergs—in a frozen land where even Eskimos feared to trod—left me with plenty of spare time. I started to think about religion. I didn't think too long, though, because I was convinced to do so would be foolish. I remained steadfast in my agnostic beliefs; yet again I can't recall anyone in the military sharing the truth of Christ with me.

The Start of My Legal Career

After completing two years, six months, and twenty-one days as a Second Lieutenant in the Air Force—not that I was counting the days—I completed my legal training at the University of San Francisco. After graduation in 1956, I joined a law firm on the Sunset Strip in Los Angeles, which was bustling from all the westward migration following World War II. Growing up in quiet Silverton hardly prepared me for the sea of asphalt and mass of humanity taking over Southern California. After only five days in L.A., I wanted out. I looked for a small town where I could start my own practice, and I found one in Indio—150 miles east of Los Angeles in the California desert. To get to Indio in those days, one had to pass through Palm Springs, which wasn't more than a few resort hotels and a handful of golf courses in the 1950s.

Then again, Palm Springs, with its Hollywood clientele and Rat Pack following, looked like a booming metropolis compared to sleepy Indio, which had more date trees than people. Still, I found a niche after hanging out my shingle as a personal injury attorney. I won my wronged clients justice and compensation, and my practice flourished. My triumphs in the courtroom begat wealth and fame, and I rather enjoyed the sweet trappings of success. Again, I can't recall anyone in my circle sharing the truth of Christ with me, but I wouldn't have listened anyway. I was too busy chasing more wealth and more fame. It didn't help to deter this chasing when the National Law Journal named me as one of the Top Ten trial lawyers in the United States and my colleagues elected me president of the California Trial Lawyers Association. That's the track I stayed on for more than twenty years.

In the summer of 1974, while attending the annual American Trial Lawyers Convention in New York City, Francis Hare, Jr., a prominent trial lawyer from Alabama and my close friend for many years, shared with me the startling proposition that the claims of Christ were verifiably true. This conversation didn't last for more than two minutes, but in that short amount of time, he explained that the prophecies written hundreds of years before the birth of Christ had actually been fulfilled by Jesus.

That's interesting, I thought. I paid attention to Francis because everyone considered him to be reliable and trustworthy. This was the first time I can remember someone sharing with me the verifiable truth of Christ.

Although Francis gave me something to think about, I still didn't want anything to do with religion. I couldn't see myself having anything in common with narrow-minded, politically conservative, and hypocritical Christians. I viewed myself as just the opposite: open-minded, socially liberally, and genuine.

I had all the arguments down in my mind:

1. Jesus was a great teacher and historical figure, but He certainly was not God of the Universe.

2. If the conduct of Christians was an example of Christ, then that wasn't for me.

3. Why, if there was only one true God, were there so many different churches?

4. All this cogitation on religion was for naught, because I had no desire to give up my lavish lifestyle.

My Biggest Case

In May 1976, I was living in Palm Springs, which had grown up to become a world-class resort. I asked an architect named

George Maclean to design a new home for me and my girlfriend, Joy, who would later become my wife. The fact that George was a world renowned architect who had designed the Acapulco Hotel in Mexico had my attention. We were sitting at my dining room table, poring over plans when he suddenly changed the subject.

"Tom, I'm a believer in Christ, and it's been amazing to me to find out that the Bible is true. I mean, you can even verify it," he said.

"Really?" I questioned, as my natural skepticism rose to the surface.

"Yes, really," George replied. "Tell you what. I'm going to give you a Bible and you can check it out."

That statement prompted a retort punctuated by several earthy expletives. I basically pointed out that what he was saying didn't make any sense and I would be glad to prove my point, just like if I was arguing a case before a jury.

"Be my guest," he said.

George, good to his word, presented me with a Bible, but as I thumbed through the ponderous prose, I couldn't help but recall the story about the late, great comedian W.C. Fields, a devout atheist. Just before his death, a friend strolled into his garden in Philadelphia and caught him reading the Bible.

Startled, his friend asked, "What are you doing reading that?"

W.C. Fields looked up and adjusted his bifocals. In his imitable voice, he declared, "I'm looking for a loophole, my friend ... looking for a loophole."

That was my mindset as I examined the Bible over the next three months. Looking for a loophole. But I never found one. I investigated the claims and prophesies made in the Bible, cross-examined statements made by witnesses who knew Jesus Christ when He trod on this earth. I double-checked as many statements as I could. In short, I employed all my courtroom experience and savvy to solve a mystery: Was Jesus Christ, in fact, the true God? In my reading of Scripture, Jesus stated many times that He was God. If He was an ordinary person, such a statement could only come from a lunatic or a liar.

This was the biggest case I would ever argue—and to a jury of one, myself. Until I was convinced that what Jesus Christ said was true, I would forever have those doubts. My reservations were washed away, though, after three months of investigation when I rendered my verdict. On September 5, 1976, at 11:20 a.m., I listened to Pastor John Emmans at the Palm Springs Community Church present the Gospel and ask those in attendance to raise their arms if they wanted to accept Jesus Christ as their Lord and Savior.

I looked to my right and then to my left, and then I slowly raised my heavy right arm with anticipation and fear in heart—fear because I wondered what I was getting into, but that fear soon turned to joy.

Among the things that were particularly pertinent to me in making this decision was that Jesus not only permitted but demanded us to cross-examine His claims. The Bible explains that it is not enough to worship Him with our heart and soul, but also with our mind. This also was persuasive to me. Thus, He not only permitted but He welcomed us to cross-examine the very claims that I had rejected in ignorance.

A Thunderbolt

Among the first people that I talked to about my faith was my cousin Bruce Wallen, who was my closest relative since I had no brothers or sisters. Although he lived in Seattle, we spent many childhood summers together in Silverton playing Monopoly, swimming, bicycling, and generally getting into harmless mischief. Since he was a few years older, I looked up to him.

I wasn't surprised when Bruce became a very successful advertising executive, working in Manhattan and living in Connecticut. He was a devoted husband and father of many. He played the trumpet, I thought, like Louis Armstrong. His only vice was alcohol, which he abused and which affected nearly every phase of his life.

After I became a believer, I told him many times how I had

investigated the claims of the Bible and found them to be true. Bruce listened politely, but he never indicated that he wanted to become a believer. I never pushed, but at the same time, I kept the discussions going. Suddenly, our of nowhere, Bruce died of cardiac arrest, and I flew back to his funeral in Connecticut. The family held a reception in their home, and I found myself absentmindedly strolling in his study as I quietly reflected on his life. Scanning his bookshelf, I noticed a thick, leather-bound Bible that had been clearly used—and read.

I opened the Bible to the first page, where a sentence had been inscribed in Bruce's hand: "Today after talking to Tommy and considering what he said, I accepted Jesus Christ into my heart."

Underneath this thunderbolt declaration was his signature and a date—one week before his unexpected heart attack! Unbridled joy leaped into my heart. Then several thoughts came to mind. What if I hadn't sent him this Bible? What if I hadn't shared with him the truths as set forth in Verdict? This personal angst would have been unbearable. The avoidance of this angst was a profound and compelling motivation for me to write Verdict.

A Decision to Publish

The book you're holding in your hands has been a labor of love—a self-published adventure since its release in 2003. In just a few years, I've distributed 4,000 copies of Verdict and heard from hundreds of readers who were touched or impacted by the book's message. My desire has been to get the book to as wide an audience as possible:

1. Atheists who deny that God exists.
2. Agnostics who just don't care.
3. Religious groups who deny the deity of Jesus.
4. Believers.

I know that many more people populate the first three categories than the fourth. Looking at my list, we'll always have people who cross their arms and say, "There is no God." I can't tell you whether atheism is in ascendancy, but it's clearly okay—even fashionable—to declare that God doesn't exist and is nothing more than an emotional crutch.

As for agnostics who just don't care, Mike Creswell in his book Christianity in Europe pointed out that we don't have to look any further than Western Europe to see how little Christianity means to these peoples today. Whereas places like Italy, France, Germany, and Great Britain flourished at one time and spread the Gospel to other lands, today they resemble spiritually dry lakebeds. In Germany, the birthplace of Martin Luther, ninety-nine out of a hundred people don't have a clue about the Gospel. Fewer yet of the Dutch can even explain what Easter means. It's generally believed that less than 1 percent of the population in Western Europe are evangelical Christians.

In France, which has been beset by unrest recently, only one-fourth of the country's 57 million people are affiliated with a church. Then again, you have to wonder how many of those are attending mosques rather than cathedrals since Muslims are 10 percent of the French population. There's no doubt that Islam is in ascendancy in Europe and Christianity is slouching toward extinction.

The reason for disinterest in Europe is because they haven't been exposed to the truth as set forth in Verdict.

A Buffet Line Mentality

Here in the United States, more people call themselves "Christians" than they do in Europe, but many pick and choose what they believe about Jesus Christ and the Bible—much like walking through a buffet line offering servings of religion a la carte. Many Americans do not have a "biblical worldview," which is comprised of six core beliefs:

1. The inerrancy of the Bible.
2. The sinless nature of Jesus Christ.
3. The literal existence of Satan.

4. The unlimited power and abounding knowledge of God.
5. The belief in salvation by grace alone.
6. The belief in the Crucifixion and Resurrection of Jesus.

The Bible teaches that belief in the Crucifixion and Resurrection of Jesus is essential for salvation (Romans 10:9) and that good works alone are not sufficient (Romans 3:28 and Titus 3:5). Yet many Christians don't know or believe that clear teaching. Author and researcher George Barna made waves by citing the following statistics based upon his well-conducted surveys of American Christians:

38 percent of people who identified themselves as "born again" said "that if a person is good enough, he or she can earn a place in heaven." In other words, belief in the Crucifixion and Resurrection of Jesus is not necessary for salvation.

31 percent of those who said they were born again believe that while Jesus lived on this earth, He committed sins like other people, which means that Jesus is not God because God is without sin.

Just 9 percent of all born-again adults possess a biblical world, view. Therefore, 91 percent do not.

Just 7 percent of Protestants possess a biblical world view. Therefore, 93 percent do not.

Barna's research organization also interviewed 601 senior pastors nationwide representing a random cross-section of Protestant churches. This survey revealed that only 51 percent of such Protestant pastors have a biblical worldview. Therefore 49 percent do not.

"The most important point," Barna argued, "is that you can't give people what you don't have."

Barna also said: "The low percentage of Christians who have a biblical worldview is a direct reflection of the fact that half of our primary religious teachers and leaders do not have one."

Barna observed: "In some denominations, the vast majority of clergy do not have a biblical worldview, and it shows up clearly in the data related to the theological views and moral choices of people who attend those churches."

Barna suggested that people do not get a biblical worldview simply by regularly attending church. "A biblical worldview must be both taught and caught - that is, it has to be explained and modeled. Clearly, there are huge segments of the Christian body that are missing the benefit of such a comprehensive and consistent expression of biblical truth."

Barna continued: "The research also points out that even in churches where the pastor has a biblical worldview, most of the congregants do not. More than six out of seven congregants in the typical church do not share the biblical worldview of their pastor even when he or she has one. This intimates that merely preaching good sermons or offering helpful programs does not enable most believers to develop a practical and scriptural theological base to shape their life."

Barna's compelling research confirmed what we already know: that it is not enough just to attend a church. You don't become a born-again believer by attending church any more than you become a car by stepping into a garage.

Presenting the Evidence

A biblical worldview will be both taught and caught from reading Verdict. This book will fill the gap of those pastors who do not teach—or worse—don't have such a biblical worldview.

I've sat in church pews and listened to pastors that I know do not believe in the inerrancy of the Bible or that Satan is alive today. Oh, they may not come right out and voice those views, but by the way they theologically beat around the bush, I can tell that their hearts aren't engaged in their preaching.

I'm no preacher, of course, but I do know how to stand up before a jury and present a case, and that's what I've done in Verdict. If you haven't experienced the consistent expression of biblical truth, then Verdict will supply a scriptural foundation that you can use to find or build your faith in Jesus Christ.

I've found that the problem isn't getting people to believe the substance of this book, but rather the impetus to first read it. Once folks start reading, incredible things happen. The following are among the many readers who formerly were either agnostics or atheists who came to Christ as a result of reading Verdict.

1. Taxi drivers
2. Scientists
3. Uninformed Christians
4. Teachers
5. Athletes
6. Students
7. Stay-at-home moms
8. And one who read my book while contemplating suicide, which he avoided by discovering the truth in Verdict.

Let me share a few of the unsolicited comments I received from readers of Verdict:

"This book is next in importance to the Bible itself for non-believers. It is legally convincing of the true identity of Jesus from exhaustive secular and biblical research in simple logical language by a very successful and formerly agnostic trial lawyer."

"Thank you for the gift of the book Verdict. It is the most exceptional book I have ever read except the Bible itself. Being a recent Christian believer (at age sixty-five, now seventy-nine), I still think frequently in learned, secular, and worldly ways. This book convinced me completely of the true exceptionalness of the Bible, truly written by God Himself. As an engineer, I needed specified facts, as you would find in equipment specifications. I needed this push into more truths to increase my Christian stability and to more persuasively convince others, like my own sons, who were raised as I was without the Word. Thank you again for this exceptional gift."

"I read Tom's book over the weekend, and I am struggling to describe my feelings. He makes a compelling case for the divinity of Jesus in a way that I obviously cannot refute. I am Jewish by upbringing (not practicing), so on the one hand, it is difficult for me to accept Jesus as divine when I have always been conditioned to believe that He is a great prophet; on the other hand, I have always been curious about the facts surrounding His resurrection. The clincher was for me that His resurrection has never been disputed. Also, the changes in His disciples after His resurrection (Paul in particular) are otherwise impossible to explain. I saw an ABC News Special about Jesus not too long ago, and this fortified my beginning to again question the Bible. Tom's explanation of the Trinity is excellent. It's the closest I've come to understanding the concept, and it has always confused me. Anyway, I could write several more pages but I have to go to work. My main point is to thank you for the book."

"While most religions and churches prompt people to say to simply go on faith, your connections between Scripture and fact are very thought-provoking. Your book offers something for everyone. For the agnostic, it certainly stimulates questions and perhaps possibilities, because it cannot be so easily dismissed. For the believers, it offers confirmation and comfort and takes them to a higher level of reason, along with their faith. For those whose faith has perhaps been diluted, it presents a life raft that may keep them afloat until safer waters return."

"The one part that absolutely struck me and offered hope, consolation, and confirmation was Tom's comment: 'There is no attempt to sanitize the record by any of the authors. It has been my experience as a trial lawyer that the credible witness is the one who relates bad things about himself forthrightly.' This is a simple, yet brilliant, statement. And it means so much coming from one who is so experienced."

"Though I am not able to offer an opinion on the Scriptures because I certainly am not qualified, the clarity, reasonableness, and factual approach you present in this book is unique and acts as a magnet for the mind, as well as the heart. I plan to spend many hours looking into it and trying to understand it from a novice point of view. You are so kind for sharing. We always take a chance when we offer something so deep about ourselves and it was very unselfish of you to do so."

Where We Go From Here

To borrow a courtroom phrase, I'm about to approach the jury box and present my case to you—the jury. I will present the evidence and make my best arguments. I'll talk about what the discovery of the Dead Sea Scrolls in 1947 means ... what the prophecies in the Old Testament were about Jesus and how they were fulfilled ... how the Bible contains prophecies regarding our future ... and the end of the age.

In a court of law, everything starts with a search for the truth. Are you going to sit on my jury and search for that truth?

Table of Contents

To Dr. Arnold G. Fruchtenbaum,
for his lectures, books, and tapes
that were foundational to this book.

ΔΩ

And one of them, a lawyer, asked Him a question, testing him, "Teacher, which is the great commandment in the Law?" And He said to him, "You shall love the Lord your God with all your heart, and all your soul, and with all your mind."

—Matthew 22:35-37, NASB

The Successful Search for Truth

1

Truth.

We all search for it. Some secretly, others more openly. Throughout the eons, philosophers have attempted to explain the universe, the origins of mankind, scientific discoveries, and even abstractions like goodness and mercy without reference to God as the source of that truth. It has been said that knowledge without God results in intellectual barbarism. It has been my experience, however, that no one—not even agnostics or atheists—can refute the truths of Jesus Christ. This is not surprising since Jesus so promised in Luke 21:15:

> "For I will give you utterance and wisdom which none of your opponents will be able to resist or refute."

Until September 5, 1976, I was engaged in a hopeless and empty search for this truth. Why was it hopeless? Why was it empty? Because I excluded Christ from that search. I finally concluded that success, as the world defined it, was not satisfying.

Purchasing a new car, winning a larger verdict, and receiving acclaim as a top attorney had proved to be unfulfilling. Previously, I was convinced that if others acknowledged me as great trial lawyer and if I became the president of the California Trial Lawyers Association, then life would be very satisfying indeed. When those events happened—I obtained several million-dollar verdicts before juries and I won election as president of the California Trial Lawyers Association—instead of being fulfilled, I continued to feel emptiness in my life. Although then and now I continue to enjoy being a trial lawyer, nothing could eliminate this void in my life, not even the excitement and challenge of being a trial lawyer at the top of his game. That's when I began searching for the truth of life. (Truthfully my initial impetus was to prove the Bible was not true, validating my agnosticism). Something far deeper than a court victory or a more expensive Mercedes was needed, which is why on the day before Labor Day in 1976, I put my trust in Jesus Christ and accepted Him into my heart.

The evidence for the deity of Christ is being presented as if you are on the jury, and I am trying the case. I intend to acquaint you with the facts concerning the deity of Jesus and let you decide who He is—just like any courtroom jury. In the courtroom prior to impaneling a jury, we have an opportunity to ask jurors questions. This procedure is called *voir dire*. The purpose of *voir dire* is to search a juror's mind concerning any prejudices or presuppositions that he or she may have concerning the subject matter to be litigated. The two questions I pose to you in *voir dire*, in an attempt to determine if you have any prejudices or presuppositions concerning the deity of Jesus Christ, are the following:

1. If it could be proved to you by solid and persuasive evidence that Jesus really is the Messiah and the Son of God, would you believe it?

2. If you reject the Bible as not being true, is that rejection based upon a study of the Bible and a conclusion on a rational basis that it is not true?

If those questions had been posed to me prior to September 5, 1976, I would have rejected them, along with anything supernatural. This was my presupposition and prejudice. I believed in a principle that Karl Marx was reputed to have said: "Religion is a simple solution for life's complex problems." I rejected the Bible as not being true, and yet I had not studied it, but looking back, I can see that this rejection came out of ignorance.

When I launched into a three-month study of the Bible in June 1976, it soon became evident to me that the claims of Jesus were founded on His *life* and not just on His ethical teachings. Jesus summarized this when He said in John 14:6:

> "I am the Way, and the Truth, and the *Life*."

And Peter said the same in 2 Peter 1:16:

> For we did not follow cleverly devised tales when we made known to you the power and coming of our Lord Jesus Christ, but we were *eyewitnesses* of his majesty.

C. S. Lewis, a professor at Oxford from 1954 to 1963 and the author of more than forty books, accepted Christ only after a thorough study of the evidence. About religion, he stated:

> "The really important question about religion is not whether it works but whether it is true."

Let me make this assertion: it will not work unless it is true.

Prior to September 5, 1976, I concluded that to become a believer in Christ, one had to leave his or her brains at the church doorstep. Certainly the claims of Christ could not withstand the scrutiny of history, archaeology, or any other relevant discipline—or even more so a scorching cross-examination from a trial lawyer like me.

To my amazement, however, I discovered that Jesus Christ not only permitted believers in Him to retain their brains, but it was His command that we determine for ourselves this truth through examining and skeptically questioning the claims of Christ. Three passages were persuasive to me in that regard, and each gave me insight into the character of our Lord. The first was when a *lawyer* attempted to trip up Jesus by pinning Him down as to what was the greatest commandment of Moses. (All references, unless otherwise noted, are from the New American Standard Bible [NASB] translation. Any italicizing done by me is to underscore the importance of words and points I want to emphasize.)

> And one of them, a *lawyer*, asked Him a question testing Him, "Teacher, which is the great commandment in the law?" And He said to him, "You shall love the Lord your God with all your heart and with all your soul and with all your *mind*."
>
> —Matthew 22:35-37

This verse is foundational for the conclusions in this book and is much like a three-legged stool, which will not stand without three legs. Neither will our relationship or our beliefs in Christ stand firm unless we love God with our hearts, our souls, and our *minds*. We will not attain the faith similar to a house built "upon the rock," as discussed by Jesus in Matthew 7:24-27, without the use of our minds. Nor will we be able to withstand the barbs of the world.

Our Lord, on the subject of truth, said this in John 8:32:

> "And you shall know the truth and the *truth* shall make you *free*."

In a discussion with Pontius Pilate just before Jesus' death, we learn this from Scripture:

> Pilate therefore said to Him, "So you are a king?" Jesus answered, "You say correctly that I am a king. For this I have been born, and for this I have come into the world, to bear witness to the *truth*. Everyone on the side of *truth* listens to me."
>
> —John 18:37, NIV

Upon reading these three passages, I became concerned and perplexed at the willingness of Jesus to allow cross-examination of the very claims that I rejected out of ignorance. Little did I know that Jesus Christ was willing to have His claims examined with our minds. Little did I know that it was a command from Christ to examine history or archaeology or any other relevant discipline and that examination would lead to the *truth* and that *truth* would lead to Christ (Colossians 1:1-12).

This challenge I accepted during my three-month study in 1976. I was motivated to find a loophole, any loophole, in the truths of Christ. Finding none, however, frightened me and finally brought me to my knees.

More than Lip Service

The Apostle Paul instructs that the thinking of believers should not be like that of children but rather *mature:*

> Brethren, do not be children in your thinking; yet in evil be babes, but in your thinking be mature.
>
> —1 Corinthians 14:20

We are instructed by the Lord regarding the use of our minds:

> "Come now, and let us reason together," says the Lord.
>
> —Isaiah 1:18

Finally, we are promised understanding in everything:

> Consider what I say, for the Lord will give you understanding in *everything*.
>
> —2 Timothy 2:7

Our Lord likewise, in Isaiah 29:13, warns us against giving Him mere lip service learned from tradition and rote, rather than our minds. Jeremiah 12:2 expresses the same thought: "Thou are near to their lips, but far from their mind."

As an aside, I discovered that Christ does not have any political predilections. Those who attempt to do so are eliminating and twisting His clear teaching. The teaching of the Bible supercedes the dictates of any political party.

The whole world, even agnostics and atheists, would like—if they are intellectually honest—to be able to determine on a rational basis the one true God. Chapter 2 sets forth God's clear and unassailable basis to determine just that.

How Prophecies Determine and Verify the One True God

2

This lesson may be the most significant one in this book. Why? Because by the standards set forth here by Isaiah, the world—and particularly unbelievers—can identify the one true God. What an unbeliever does with his or her life after concluding that the God of the Bible is the one true God is another matter, however.

According to biblical scholars, approximately 25 percent of the Bible consists of prophecies. The penalty for a Jewish prophet if he was wrong was death (Deuteronomy 18:20). Prophets often wrote near- and far-term prophecies. Near-term prophecies required fulfillment within the lifetime of the hearers so that they could verify its truth, and thereby conclude that the far-term prophecies would likewise be reliable. The Jewish prophet, Isaiah, *established prophecies* as being the *test* for determining the one true God:

> "*Present your case*," the Lord says. "Bring forward your strong *arguments*," the King of Jacob says. Let them bring forth and declare to us *what is going to take place*; as for the former events, declare what they were, that we may consider them, and know their outcome; or announce to us what is

> coming. Declare the things that are going to come afterward, that we may know *that you are gods*.
>
> —Isaiah 41:21-23b

Isaiah explained that *only* God can so prophesy in Isaiah 41:26:

> Who has declared this from the beginning, that we might know? Or from former times, that we may say, "He is right!"? Surely there was *no one* who declared, surely there was no one who proclaimed, surely there was *no one* who heard your words.

Isaiah also set forth that God has not and *will not* share this gift of prophecy with anyone in Isaiah 42:8-9:

> "I am the Lord, that is My name; *I will not give My glory* to another, nor My praise to graven images.
>
> "Behold, the former things have come to pass, now I declare new things; before they spring forth I proclaim them to you."

Isaiah 44:6-8 challenges those who *claim* to be God to act like God and prophesy like God:

> "Thus says the Lord, the King of Israel and his Redeemer, the Lord of hosts; 'I am the first and I am the last, and there is no God besides Me. Who is like Me? *Let him proclaim* and declare it; yes, *let him recount* it to Me in order, from the time that I established the ancient nation. And *let them declare* to them the things that are coming. And the events that are going to take place. Do not tremble and do not be afraid; have I not long since announced it to you and declared it? And you are My witnesses. Is there any God besides Me, or is there any other Rock? I know of none.' "

Isaiah additionally explained that *no one except God can declare* "things which have not been done" in Isaiah 46:8-10b:

> "Remember this, and be assured; recall it to mind, you transgressors. Remember the former things long past for I am God, and there is no other; I am God, and there is *no one like* Me, declaring the *end* from the *beginning* and from *ancient times things which have not been done*."

The following passage explains that prophecies will prevent idols and graven images, or any belief system that is at variance with the Bible, from obtaining any glory. Also, this passage acknowledges what we all intuitively know: that *believers* are in need of such prophecies to remain steadfast in our beliefs and to prevent our faith from being successfully attacked by the world. *Unbelievers* need such prophecies to reach the conclusion that Jesus is the Messiah.

> "I *declared the former things long ago* and they went forth from My mouth, and I proclaimed them. Suddenly I acted, and *they came to pass*. Because I know that you are *obstinate*, and your *neck is an iron sinew*, and your *forehead bronze*, therefore *I declared them to you long ago*, before they took place I proclaimed them to you, lest you should say, 'My *idol has done them*, and my *graven image* and my molten image have commanded them.'
>
> "You have heard; look at all this. And you, will you not declare it? I proclaim to you new things from this time, even hidden things which you have not known.
>
> "They are created now and not long ago; and before today you have not heard them, lest you should say, 'Behold, I knew them.' "
>
> —Isaiah 48:3-7

In sum, Isaiah sets forth the test for identifying the true God as the ability *to announce what is coming*. Also, he explained that God will not share this gift with anyone. The prophecies of God's Word are not right just some of the time, but they are right all of the time. These prophecies did not predict that it would rain a week from Tuesday, but rather they foretold with specificity and accuracy events of an entire nation such as Israel, Russia, Ethiopia, Germany, Armenia, Iran, Somalia, Phoenicia, Egypt, Sidon, Syria and Babylon, among others. These prophecies also foretold specific events to occur in the future concerning Jesus the Messiah.

In John 13:19, Jesus related the same teaching as Isaiah 48:3-7:

> "From now on I am telling you before it comes to pass, so that when it does occur, *you may believe that I am He*."

This verse also establishes that Jesus clearly understood the persuasiveness of prophecies.

Peter explained what common sense dictates, which is that all prophesying must be from God:

> But know this first of all, that no prophecy of Scripture is a matter of one's own interpretation, for no prophecy was ever made by an act of human will, but men moved by the Holy Spirit spoke from God.
>
> —2 Peter 1:20-21

Jesus understood that His disciples needed these prophecies to sustain their faith and even more so for present-day believers and unbelievers when He explained to His disciples in John 14:29:

> "And now I have told you before it comes to pass, that when it comes to pass, *you may believe*."

So what have we learned about indentifying the one true

God, that even atheists and agnostics, if intellectually honest, must agree with? Answer—that *only* the one true God could prophecy "what is going to take place." A *false god will always fail this profound test*. Thus, God makes it so simple for the entire world to understand and *unerringly identify* the one true God, which our proof will establish is the God of the Bible.

As God indicated, whenever the world attempts to predict the future, the results are almost laughable if not pathetic. In the *Miami Herald* on January 3, 1990, the following was written regarding those "predictions" made by psychics during 1989:

> **For Psychics, 1989 Was Too Unpredictable**
>
> In the realm of psychic predictions, 1989 was a year when the Berlin Wall fell ten years too soon, Manuel Noriega blew a mid-life career change, and Zsa Zsa Gabor got three days instead of eternal salvation. Here are 1989's biggest flops: Jeane Dixon almost won her own room and wax statue in the Psychic Hall of Fame by predicting that the Berlin Wall would be sold brick by brick for souvenirs.
>
> Which happened. But not in the 21st century, as she said it would. And in psychic predictions and pregnancies, almost doesn't count. The phone also rang for two *National Examiner* forecasters, but they didn't have call waiting. One predicted that Noriega would flee Panama and move to New York, where he would become a model for a pineapple juice distributor. Another sensed major changes for Zsa Zsa but predicted she would join Hare Krishna.
>
> Nobody in the scandal sheets saw the San Francisco earthquake coming. Or the upheaval in China. Or the invasion of Panama. Instead, the *National Enquirer's* 10 Leading Psychics foresaw a jetliner crashing into the Vatican, Roseanne Barr on a diet, Jane Fonda getting fat, and Madonna having a baby.

> Other big busts: Ronald and Nancy Reagan were to take over PTL from Jim and Tammy Bakker, which to our knowledge they have not yet done. Negotiations hung up over rights to the water slide. President Bush [No. 1] was to force the White House press corps to take classes in good manners. New York's Statue of Liberty was supposed to fall over. Instead, Ed Koch did. Soviet leader Mikhail Gorbachev was to defect to the United States; Nadia Comaneci got the jump on him. A French psychic was to astound the world with a mind transfer demonstration that produced a talking cat. Tragedy was to follow, however: the fleeing feline was to be struck dead by a bus, leaving the psychic meowing for life.

An update on the reliability of psychic prophecies appeared in the *Los Angeles Times* on January 2, 1998:

> **Predictably, Psychics Botch '97 Forecasts**
>
> Buffalo, N.Y. (AP) Had the psychics been right, 1997 would have gone down in history as the year rocker Mick Jagger became a member of Parliament and former television anchorman Walter Cronkite a critically acclaimed lounge singer.
>
> O.J. Simpson would be a big star on French television as the host of a "whodunit" show, and actor John Travolta a hero for landing a commercial jetliner when its crew came down with food poisoning. Princess Diana would be alive too, although either weighing 215 pounds because of a thyroid ailment or living in Africa while training as an Olympic long-distance runner, depending on which psychic you believed.
>
> There was little—make that nothing—that

the psychics got right in their predictions for the *National Enquirer, National Examiner,* and other tabloids. So says the *Skeptical Inquirer.* The magazine published in the Buffalo suburb of Amherst said it applies scientific method to claims of the paranormal. The psychics' collective strikeout came as no surprise to Gene Emery, who has been checking the forecasts for the magazine since 1979.

"They are consistent," he said. Since 1979, Emery has found only one prediction that came half-true. That was in 1993, when a *National Enquirer* psychic said Florida would be hit hard by an earthquake weeks after being devastated by the worst hurricane in state history. The timing of the forecast was right for Hurricane Andrew, but there was no temblor.

Among other predictions for 1997:

• Barbra Streisand was to convert Rush Limbaugh into a liberal Democrat.

• Pamela Anderson Lee was to either become a Washington lobbyist or star with Howard Stern in a rock musical version of *Gone With the Wind.*

• Sarah Ferguson was to join the cast of "Melrose Place" and marry Calvin Klein.

• Madonna, concerned about the quality of children's television shows, was to revive the Mickey Mouse Club and cast herself as its star. Emery, who also writes a column for the *Skeptical Inquirer,* said he keeps track of the psychic flops to prove a point. "I do this as an annual reality check to people who really want to know whether these folks have any talent," he said, "and it's become clear over the years that they don't."

Some may be tempted to toast what did not happen as they say goodbye to 1997. Kathie Lee Gifford might have attracted more tabloid attention

> than she cared to. But at least she wasn't abducted by aliens and dropped to wander for five weeks in the Colorado wilderness as one soothsayer predicted.
>
> Undaunted by their 1997 misses, the psychics already are polishing their crystal balls for 1998. Look for a cure for the common cold, a drink for nighttime joggers that will make their skin glow in the dark, and the need to kill all cats to stop the spread of a virus that blinds humans.
>
> And then look for Emery's column.

Chapter 3 distinguishes the Bible from all other books. Authors, scientists, archeologists, and historians are in awe of the Bible for reasons I'll discuss in the next two-page chapter.

The Bible: Its Uniqueness and Reliability

3

The Bible should be judged by the same standard that we would judge any other book. There should be no presupposition that it is either true or false.

In comparison with all other books, the Bible is unique. It was written over a period of 1,600 years, in sixty-six books, by forty authors. These authors came from all walks of life. Two of them were half-brothers of Jesus Christ who did not believe His claims until after they witnessed His Crucifixion and Resurrection. The Bible was written in different locations, including the thrones of kings and the dungeons of castles; on three different continents—Asia, Africa and Europe; and in three different languages, Aramaic, Hebrew, and Greek. In spite of the diversity of its authors and being written over such a long period—and that most of the authors did not have access to the other authors' writings—the Bible displays a consistency in facts as well as theology. Not one author criticized another. There are no dissenting opinions or footnotes.

Archaeologists, when in Israel, rely on the Bible to determine the location of tells, or sites, which has proved to be unerringly accurate. Historians have long acknowledged the Bible's trustworthiness.

The next chapter discusses the Dead Sea Scrolls, which were discovered in 1947. This discovery made shambles of the arguments made by antagonists that the Bible was unreliable.

The Dead Sea Scrolls

4

Because the Bible was transcribed many times over thousands of years, critics claimed it was transcribed inaccurately and therefore not reliable. Prior to 1947, the oldest known complete Bible was transcribed in 900 A.D. Even though the Jewish scribes were well disciplined and ritualistic in transcribing the Bible, it was nevertheless alleged that they must have transcribed it inaccurately.

In 1947, a Bedouin shepherd lost a goat near the Dead Sea. He saw this goat standing on a ledge. To retrieve the goat from the ledge, he threw rocks at it. Some of these rocks landed in an adjacent cave. The shepherd could hear the rocks breaking jars. Upon closer examination, he observed in this cave broken and unbroken jars. Located in these jars were what we now know as the Dead Sea Scrolls, which contained portions of all the books of the Hebrew Scriptures, with the exception of the Book of Esther, but including the entire book of Isaiah. Paleographers determined the Dead Sea Scrolls were transcribed at least 125 years before Jesus' birth. Comparison of the Dead Sea Scrolls with the Bible that was transcribed in 900 A.D. revealed that the Bible transcription in 900 A.D. was 96 percent consistent with the Dead Sea

Scrolls. The remaining 4 percent of material was primarily mistakes in spelling.

Time magazine, in its August 14, 1989 edition, stated:

> The scrolls have also affected Bible translations read by millions of Jews and Christians. The caves contained portions of all books of the Old Testament except Esther, including a remarkably complete scroll of Isaiah that is 1,000 years older than any other surviving manuscript. Besides clearing up anomalies in several verses, the scrolls have demonstrated the *remarkable accuracy* with which Jewish scribes preserved the text of the Bible.

In *Biblical Archaeology Review* (December 1992), an article by two *Jewish* scholars concerning the Dead Sea Scrolls stated:

> Our Qumran text, 4Q521, is astonishingly, quite close to this Christian concept of the Messiah. Our text speaks not only of a single Messianic figure . . . but it also describes Him in extremely exalted terms, *quite like the Christian view of Jesus* as a cosmic agent. That there was, in fact, an expectation of a single Messianic figure at Qumran is really not so surprising.
>
> In short, there is not much evidence in the previously published scrolls that straightforwardly supports a putative doctrine of two Messiahs . . . So the text that is the subject of this article (4Q521) is, in speaking of a single Messiah, more the rule than the exception . . . The Messiah of our text is thus much closer to the Christian Messiah, in this regard, than in any previously published text and requires us to reexamine the previously, rather restricted, views of Messianic expectations at Qumran.

Therefore, the argument that had previously been made—that the Messianic prophecies were so accurate that they had to have been written *after* the first advent of Christ—was shattered because paleographers established that the Dead Sea Scrolls were transcribed at least 125 years before the first advent of Christ.

God utilized the Jewish people for many purposes, including being used as conduits for prophecies concerning historical events that would be fulfilled by them hundreds of years later. Through these fulfillments, it will be established yet again that only God could so prophesy, as our next chapter establishes.

Prophecies Concerning the Jewish People and Israel

5

Because of the Jewish people's disobedience (Leviticus 26:19), God, through Moses, prophesied that their cities and sanctuaries would become desolate:

> "I will *lay waste your cities* as well, and will make your *sanctuaries desolate;* and I will not smell your soothing aromas. And I will make the *land desolate* so that your enemies who settle in it shall be *appalled* over it. You, however, I will scatter among the nations and will draw out a sword after you, as your land becomes *desolate* and your cities become *waste*."
>
> —Leviticus 26:31-33

Moses wrote Leviticus around 1500 to 1400 B.C., over 700 years before his prophecies were fulfilled. In analyzing this prophecy and its fulfillment, we find the following:

• **Point 1:** Verse 33 says, "You, however, I will scatter among the nations." This prophecy, as verified in the *Encyclopedia Britannica*, was fulfilled some 700 years later in 733-721 B.C., when Assyria captured the Northern Kingdom (then known as

Israel), which consisted of Gilead, Galilee, and Samaria. This was where the ten northern tribes lived. Assyria took them into captivity, thus scattering them and resulting in the fulfillment of "You, however, I will *scatter* among the nations":

> The westward push of the Neo-Assyrian Empire in the mid-8th century BCE soon brought Aram and Israel to their knees. In 733-732, Assyria took Gilead and Galilee from Israel and captured Aramaean Damascus; in 721 Samaria, the Israelite capital, fell. The northern kingdom sought to survive through alliances with Assyria and Egypt; its kings came and went in rapid succession.
> —*Encyclopedia Britannica,* volume 10, page 309

The fulfillment of this prophecy by the Assyrians when they carried Israel (the Northern Kingdom) into exile is also recorded in 2 Kings 17:6.

The prophecy in verse 33 that Israel would be scattered was also fulfilled in 586 B.C. when Babylon captured the Southern Kingdom (known as Judah), which contained the tribes of Judah and Benjamin as well as the city of Jerusalem. This was also verified in *Encyclopedia Britannica* (volume 10, page 309), which says:

> In 586 B.C., the doom prophecies of Jeremiah and Ezekiel came true. Rebellious Jerusalem was reduced by Nebuchadnezzar, the temple was burnt, and much of Judah's population was *dispersed* or *deported* to Babylonia.

The fulfillment of this prophecy by the Babylonians, when they carried Judah (the Southern Kingdom) into exile, is also recorded in 2 Kings 25:11.

• **Point 2.** Verse 33 also says, "So that your enemies who *settle in it* shall be appalled over it." This prophecy was fulfilled beginning in 40 B.C. when the Romans, who were "enemies" of the Jews" settled in Israel.

• **Point 3.** Verse 31 says, "And will make your *sanctuaries* desolate . . ." This prophecy was fulfilled when the temple and sanctuary was desecrated in 63 B.C. and destroyed in 70 A.D., which was also verified in the *Encyclopedia Britannica*, which said:

> "The most important religious institution of the Jews, until its *destruction in 70*, was the temple in Jerusalem—the second temple, erected 538-516 B.C. Though services were interrupted for three years by Antiochus Epiphanes (167-165 B.C.) and though the Roman General Pompey *desecrated* the temple (63 B.C.), Herod lavished great expense in rebuilding it."
>
> —*Encyclopedia Britannica*, volume 10, page 311

• **Point 4.** Verse 33 additionally says, "I will *lay waste* your *cities*." This prophecy was fulfilled in 70 A.D. when Rome laid to waste Jerusalem, as verified in the *Encyclopedia Britannica*, which said:

> "The last procurators in particular were indifferent to Jewish religious sensibilities; and various patriotic groups, to whom nationalism was an integral part of their religion, succeeded in polarizing the Jewish population and bringing on an extremely *bloody war* with Rome in 66-70. The climax of the war was the *destruction of the temple* in 70, though, according to Josephus, the Roman General (and later Emperor) Titus sought to spare it."
>
> —*Encyclopedia Britannica*, volume 10, page 315

In the continuing prophecy by Moses concerning the Jewish people, he prophesied in Deuteronomy 28:64, "Moreover, the Lord will scatter you among all peoples, from one end of the earth to the other end of the earth," which was fulfilled in 733-721 B.C. and 586 B.C., and as we have seen was verified in the *Encyclopedia Britannica*.

Ezekiel, around 570 B.C., prophesied that the Jewish people, after being scattered, would return to Israel twice (For the second gathering see page 114). The first gathering would be "with wrath poured out":

> "And I *shall bring you* out from the peoples and *gather you* from the lands where you are *scattered*, with a mighty hand and with an outstretched arm and *with wrath poured out*."
>
> —Ezekiel 20:34

This wrath will be experienced during the Tribulation as described in Revelation chapters 6-19.

> "For I will take you from the nations, *gather you* from all the lands, and bring you into your own land."
>
> —Ezekiel 36:24

The fulfillment of these prophecies in Ezekiel occurred when the Jews did return to Israel, culminating on May 14, 1948, when Israel was declared a sovereign state.

God Prophesied that the Jews Would Never Be Destroyed

God also prophesied and promised His chosen people that they would endure forever and never lose their identity:

> "For just as the new heavens and the new earth which I make will *endure* before Me," declares the Lord, "so your offspring and your name will *endure*."
>
> —Isaiah 66:22

The same prophecy that the Jewish people "are not consumed" is in Malachi 3:6:

> "For I, the Lord *do not change*; therefore you, O sons of Jacob, are *not consumed*."

The following quotations are from *Jesus Was a Jew* by Dr. Arnold Fruchtenbaum, and they concern the prophecies that the Jews would "endure":

> Such philosophers of history as Oswald Spengler and Arnold Toynbee have found themselves at a

loss to explain the Jews. Max I. Dimont points this out in his book entitled *Jews, God, and History* on page 20:

> Since the history of the Jews did not fit into either Spengler's or Toynbee's system, Spengler ignored them and Toynbee reduced them to an occasional footnote describing the Jews as fossils of history.

Philosophers of history without biblical knowledge and basing their conclusions upon non-biblical presuppositions find it impossible to explain this Jewish survival. For example, Mark Twain wrote in *Concerning the Jews* on page 281:

> The Egyptian, the Babylonian, and the Persian rose, filled the planet with sound and splendor, then faded to dream stuff and passed away; the Greek and the Roman followed, and made a vast noise, and they are gone; other peoples have sprung up and held their torch high for a time, but it burned out, and they sit in twilight, or have vanished. The Jew saw them all, beat them all, and is now what he always was, exhibiting no decadence, no infirmities of age, no weakening of his parts, no slowing of his energies, no dulling of his alert and aggressive mind. *All things are mortal but the Jew;* all other forces pass, but he remains. What is the secret of his immortality?

The Communist historian, Nicholas Berdyaev, wrote concerning the survival of the Jews in *The Meaning of History* on pages 86-87:

> According to the materialistic criterion, this people ought long ago to have perished. Its survival is a mysterious and wonderful phenomenon demonstrating that the life of this people is governed by a special predetermination, transcending the processes of adoption expounded by the materialistic interpretation of history. The survival of the Jews . . . their endurance under absolutely peculiar conditions and the fateful role played by them in history; all these point to the peculiar and mysterious foundations of their destiny.

The answer to these astonishments by authors, philosophers, and historians is found in the prophecy of Isaiah where God promises, "So your offspring and your name will endure," and in the prophecy of Malachi, where He says that the sons of Jacob "are not consumed."

By far the more populous nations at the time of Isaiah and Malachi were such people as the Hittites and Philistines. However, who has ever heard of a Russian Hittite or a German Philistine? But who has not heard of a Russian Jew or a German Jew?

John F. Kennedy was born in Brookline, Massachusetts. His father was Joseph Kennedy, and his mother was Rose Fitzgerald. Thousands of witnesses saw him assassinated in Dallas, Texas, in 1963. Now, imagine if a book were written 500 to 1,500 years before John F. Kennedy was even born, prophesying that he would be born in Brookline, Massachusetts; that his father would be Joseph Kennedy; that his mother would be Rose Fitzgerald; and that he would be assassinated in Dallas, Texas in 1963.

Would you want to know more about the author who prophesied these events 500 to 1,500 years before their occurrence? Would you want to know where he got such insight to make such prophecies?

Our next chapter, Chapter 6 establishes that God did prophesy in a similar manner concerning Jesus the Messiah. Such could only be by God. For atheist or agnostics to successfully support their beliefs, the messianic prophecies described in the next chapter must be refuted. To date, I've never heard of anyone even trying to dispute their fulfillment.

Messianic Prophecies

The objective standard to determine if Jesus is the Messiah is based on His fulfillment of the Messianic prophecies. If He did, He is, and if He did not, He is not. There must be a fulfillment of all such prophecies, not just a select few. If Jesus did not so fulfill *all* of them, He would be *disqualified* from being the Messiah and the Son of God. One miss and Jesus Christ would be disqualified.

Contained within the Hebrew Scriptures are over 300 prophecies concerning the Messiah that were fulfilled by Jesus the Messiah. These prophecies were written anywhere from 450 to over 2,000 years before the birth of Jesus. They were so vivid and clear in their fulfillment that before the discovery of the Dead Sea Scrolls, it was argued by antagonists that ordinary men could not have written them. These antagonists felt if they were written before the birth of Jesus, it, with certainty, would have required a supernatural origin. Such skeptics flatly denied anything supernatural. The Dead Sea Scrolls, as we saw in chapter 4, established *with this certainty* that all of these prophecies were written hundreds of years before the birth of Jesus. Their very argument proves the supernatural origin of these prophecies. Only a select few of them will be discussed.

Born of a Virgin

> Therefore the Lord Himself will give you a *sign:* Behold, a *virgin* will be with child and bear a son, and she will call His name *Immanuel*.
>
> —Isaiah 7:14

Ptolemy Philadelphus, a Greek ruler around 285 B.C., commissioned seventy Jewish rabbis to transcribe the Hebrew Scriptures from Hebrew and Aramaic to Greek. This work was called the Septuagint. These seventy scholars transcribed the Hebrew word *almah* to the Greek word *parthenos*, both meaning *virgin*. Many current rabbis claim the word *almah* means "young woman." Isaiah 7:14 explains that it was intended to be a "sign" so that Immanuel's identity could be determined. If it meant "young woman," some sign! Millions of young Jewish women gave birth to babies.

True God and True Man

Isaiah wrote in Isaiah 9:6-7:

> For a child will be born to us, a son will be given to us; and the government will rest upon His shoulders; and His name will be called *Wonderful, Counselor, Mighty God, Eternal Father*, Prince of Peace.
>
> There will be no end to the increase of His government or of peace. On the *throne* of David and over his kingdom, to establish it and to uphold it with justice and righteousness from then on and *forevermore*. The zeal of the Lord of hosts will accomplish this.

This passage describes prophetically that the Messiah would be *true God* and *true man*. That He would be true God is prophesied in verse 6, where it refers to Him as "*Mighty God, Eternal Father.*" This same Messiah was prophesied in verse 7 as being true man because the Messiah would sit on the throne of David "forevermore."

This requires a worldly reign. Isaiah wrote his prophecies 700 years before the birth of Jesus and before Isaiah or anyone at that time had ever heard of Jesus or His crucifixion. (See page 137 for this proof.)

Born in Bethlehem

The Jewish prophet Micah wrote in Micah 5:2 concerning the birth of the Messiah:

> But as for you, *Bethlehem* Ephrathah, too little to be among the clans of Judah, from you One will go forth from Me to be ruler of Israel. His goings forth are from long ago, *from the days of eternity*.

Only God exists eternally. Here, Micah prophesied approximately 700 years before the birth of Jesus that "one" would be born in Bethlehem who had actually existed from "*the days of eternity*." There was a problem in fulfilling this prophecy through Mary and Joseph because they lived in Nazareth. Therefore, some time before Jesus was born, they had to travel from Nazareth to Bethlehem. Continually looking for loopholes, I, as an agnostic, reasoned that Mary and Joseph, to deceive us, intentionally went to Bethlehem after reading this prophecy, resulting in its fulfillment. After all, this was a well-known prophecy to all Jews.

However, the Bible as well as other history books (the Bible is also a history book), record that Mary and Joseph's traveling to Bethlehem was not voluntary. Caesar Augustus, a pagan and ruler of Rome, required that all twelve Jewish tribes were to report to twelve *separate* cities, with the tribe of Judah reporting to Bethlehem, for the onerous purpose of taking a census so they could be taxed. One of the greatest historians, Dr. Luke, verifies this in Luke 2:1-5:

> Now it came about in those days that a decree went out from Caesar Augustus, that a census be

> taken of all the inhabited earth. This was the first census taken while Quirinius was governor of Syria.
>
> And all were proceeding to register for the census, everyone to his *own city*. [There were twelve.] And Joseph also went up from Galilee, from the city of Nazareth, to Judea, to the city of David, which is called *Bethlehem*, because he was of the *house and family of David* [tribe of Judah]. In order to register, along with Mary, who was engaged to him, and was with child.

In 1923 at Ankara, Turkey, a Roman inscription was discovered recording that there were three great censuses initiated during the reign of Caesar Augustus, the middle one occurring in 7 B.C. History also records that there were petitions sent to Rome by the Jews protesting that they had to travel this long distance for a census and worse yet, taxed.

Due to this protest there was a delay of approximately three years before this edict was carried out, resulting in the census being taken in 4 B.C. That is the precise year that Jesus was born in Bethlehem. Jesus being born in the year 4 B.C. sounds strange, but the best studies so conclude. There were a total of *twelve different cities* to which the Jews were required to go to for the purpose of taking this census and being taxed. This was verified in the passage from Luke, which states "and all were proceeding to register for the census everyone to his own city." Therefore, the prophet Micah, if not from God, had one chance out of twelve to guess the correct city where Jesus, being of the tribe of Judah (House of David) would be born.

The last sentence of Micah 5:2 describes who was to be born in Bethlehem: "His goings forth are from long ago, from the days of *eternity*." No one but God has existed "from the days of eternity." Thus this is a prophecy that God, Himself, would be born in Bethlehem and that He would be true God and true man. When Micah wrote this prophecy, Bethlehem Ephrathah was the classical name for the city of Bethlehem. This was the same as describing Palm Springs as being in California.

Entered Jerusalem on a Donkey (Palm Sunday)

Zechariah, approximately 500 years before Jesus' birth, prophesied in Zechariah 9:9:

> Rejoice greatly, O daughter of Zion! Shout in triumph, O daughter of Jerusalem! Behold, your king is coming to you; He is just and endowed with salvation, humble, and mounted on a *donkey*, even on a colt, the foal of a donkey.

The fulfillment of the above prophecy is well known when Jesus, the Messiah, entered Jerusalem mounted on a donkey, also utilizing a colt, on Palm Sunday (Matthew 21:1-6).

Isaiah 52:13-53:12

One of the most profound Messianic prophecies was written by Isaiah approximately 700 years before the birth of Jesus in Isaiah 52:13-53:12. This prophecy speaks of the Servant of Jehovah who would undergo great suffering, who would die as a result of being pierced, who would vicariously suffer this death for His people, and would be resurrected from the dead. This prophecy clearly describes in detail the suffering, death, and resurrection of Jesus the Messiah. Because of the importance of this prophecy, an analysis of it is in order on a phrase-by-phrase basis.

Resurrected and Marred

> Behold, My servant will prosper, He will be high and *lifted up*, and greatly exalted. Just as many were astonished at you, My people, so His appearance was *marred* more than any man, and His form more than the sons of men.

> Thus He will sprinkle many nations, kings will shut their mouths on account of Him; for what had not been told them they will see, and what they had not heard they will understand.
>
> —Isaiah 52:13-15

In the above prophecy, Isaiah speaks of the suffering servant being "lifted up," thus prophesying that He would be *resurrected.* In verse 14, the suffering servant who is resurrected is further identified as being "marred more than any man," and Yeshua, the Christ, was marred more "than any man" when He was scourged (whipped), crowned with thorns, and nails pierced His body (John 19:3).

Few Will Believe Him

> Who has believed our message? And to whom has the arm of the Lord been revealed?
>
> —Isaiah 53:1

During Jesus' life, very few believed in His message, thus fulfilling this prophecy. The phrase "the arm of the Lord" implies the Son of God and asks the question: to whom has the Son of God been revealed?

Virgin Birth

> For He [Jesus] grew up before Him [God the Father] like a tender shoot, and like a root out of *parched* ground.
>
> —Isaiah 53:2

This verse speaks of Yeshua's (Jesus') childhood and discusses this "root" growing up out of "parched ground," which is another description of His virgin birth. It is miraculous for a root to grow out of parched ground, just as it is miraculous for the Messiah to be born of "her seed" as set forth in Genesis 3:15. Yeshua was the only person so born of a woman's seed. Mankind is always born of a man's seed, not a woman's. The pronoun "He" refers to the Messiah, and the pronoun "Him" refers to God the Father.

No Stately Form or Majesty

Continuing with Isaiah 53:2:

> He has *no stately form or majesty* that we should look upon Him, nor appearance that we should be *attracted* to Him.

Jesus would have no "stately form or majesty" being born in a stable, being raised in Nazareth, which was so unimportant it was never mentioned in the Hebrew Scriptures, and working in His youth as a carpenter. Having no "stately form" implies that He would be a Jewish man indistinguishable from thousands of other Jewish men. This is confirmed in Mark 14:44 when, before the Crucifixion, Judas had to identify Jesus to the horde by a kiss in the Garden of Gethsemane because His "appearance" was indistinguishable from other Jewish men.

Humble

> Behold your king is coming to you; He is just and endowed with salvation. *Humble*, mounted on a *donkey*, even on a colt, the foal of a donkey.
>
> —Zechariah 9:9

Although not found in Isaiah, this prophecy confirms Jesus' humility. Kings do not ride donkeys, they ride chariots. Jesus, described as a humble servant in our Zechariah passage, fulfilled this prophecy on Palm Sunday when He entered Jerusalem on a donkey (John 12:12-14). In the first advent of Jesus Christ, He was to come as a suffering servant and not as a conquering King. In the second advent of Christ at the end of the Tribulation, just before the Messianic Kingdom, He will return—this time as a conquering King (Matthew 24:29-31). It was the failure to understand this distinction that led to considerable confusion concerning Jesus Christ, particularly by the Jews.

Despised and Forsaken: The Social Life of the Messiah

> He was *despised* and *forsaken* of men, a man of sorrows, and acquainted with grief; and like one from whom men hide their face, He was despised, and we did not esteem Him.
>
> —Isaiah 53:3

This prophecy describes the social life of Jesus the Messiah. The prophecy that He would be "forsaken of men" was vividly fulfilled in Matthew 26:56 when Jesus' disciple, Matthew, admitted that upon Jesus' arrest in the Garden of Gethsemane, he and the other disciples "left Him and fled." Throughout the Bible, the authors confess their shortcomings and sins. There is no attempt to sanitize the record by any of the authors. It has been my experience as a trial lawyer that the credible witness is the one who relates bad things about himself forthrightly.

Message of the Cross

Isaiah 53:4-6, 10c, 11d, and 12e reflect the message of the Cross that the Messiah would be the Lamb of God who would take away the sins of the world by causing all the sins of the world to fall upon Him:

> Surely our griefs He Himself *bore*, and our sorrows He carried; yet we ourselves esteemed Him stricken, smitten of God, and afflicted.
>
> But He was *pierced* through for our transgressions,

> He was *crushed* for our iniquities; the chastening for our well-being fell upon Him, and by His *scourging* we are healed.
>
> All of us like sheep have gone astray, each of us has turned to his own way; but the Lord has caused the iniquity of us all to *fall on Him*.
>
> If He would render Himself as a *guilt* offering, My servant, will justify the many. Yet He, Himself, *bore* the sin of many.

Again, the message of the Cross, this time by Zechariah:

> And I will pour out on the house of David and on the inhabitants of Jerusalem, the Spirit of grace and of supplication, so that they will look on Me whom they have *pierced;* and they will *mourn* for Him, as one mourns for an only son, and they will *weep* bitterly over Him, like the bitter weeping over a firstborn [which Jesus was].
>
> —Zechariah 12:10

The above prophecies were fulfilled when Jesus' body was "pierced" and "crushed" by being nailed to the cross and scourged by the Roman soldiers. This whipping by the Roman soldiers consisted of lashing Jesus' body with a whip made of approximately forty strands of leather, at the end of which were pieces of glass. Many died from this scourging alone.

Silent When Accused

Isaiah also prophesied that the suffering servant would humbly submit to unjust treatment and would not speak a word in His defense:

> He was oppressed and He was afflicted, yet He did *not open His mouth;* like a *lamb* that is led to slaughter, and like a sheep that is silent before its

shearers, so He did not open His mouth.

—Isaiah 53:7

The fulfillment of the above prophecy as described in the New Testament:

> Then Pilate said to Him, "Do You not hear how many things they testify against You?" And He *did not answer* him with regard to even a *single charge*, so that the governor was quite amazed.
>
> —Matthew 27:13-14

Whenever accusations were made against Jesus He never answered a "single charge" in fulfillment of this prophecy.

Judgment by Oppression

> By *oppression* and judgment He was taken away.
>
> —Isaiah 53:8a

It was prophesied that when the Messiah would be judged and crucified it would be by "oppression." Studies have established that the trial of Jesus was by oppression because Jewish law was violated in seventeen particulars. (I discuss this in *The Trial of Jesus Was By Oppression* on page 142.)

His Grave Was Assigned with the Wicked, But He Would Be Buried in a Rich Man's Tomb

Perhaps the most compelling and convincing prophecy in Isaiah to me, when I was an agnostic, was the following, written 700 years before the birth of Jesus:

> His grave was assigned with *wicked men*.
> Yet He was with a *rich man* in His death.
>
> —Isaiah 53:9

Jesus' grave was assigned to be with wicked men because He was destined to be buried with the two thieves who were crucified on either side of Him, in a common burial plot outside Jerusalem set aside exclusively for "wicked men." Was Jesus buried in this grave with "wicked men," or was He with a "rich man" in His death? The answer is found in Matthew, where Joseph of Arimathea, a "rich man," asked Pontius Pilate for the body of Jesus and thus prevented Him from being buried in a grave with "wicked men." This rich man then took the body of Jesus and buried Him in his tomb:

> And when it was evening, there came a *rich man* from Arimathea, named Joseph, who himself had also become a *disciple* of Jesus. This man came to Pilate and asked for the body of Jesus. Then Pilate ordered it to be given over to him.
>
> And Joseph took the body and wrapped it in a clean linen cloth, and laid it in his *own new tomb*, which he had hewn out in the rock; and he rolled a large stone against the entrance of the tomb and went away.
>
> —Matthew 27:57-60

God the Father Was Pleased to Offer His Son Jesus as a Guilt Offering

Isaiah prophesied that God the Father so loved the world (John 3:16) that He was pleased to render the suffering servant as a guilt offering for the sins of the people:

> But the Lord was pleased to crush Him, putting Him to grief; if He would render himself as a guilt offering; He will *see* His offspring, He will *prolong* His days and the good pleasure of the Lord will prosper in his hand.
>
> —Isaiah 53:10

The above prophecy foretells that the suffering servant would render Himself as a "guilt offering," would be crushed to death, and would thereafter be resurrected from the dead: "He will *see* His offspring, He will *prolong* his days." The only way He would *see* His offspring after being killed as a guilt offering was by being *resurrected* from the dead.

Jesus Would Willingly and Voluntarily Die for Our Sins

The next prophecy about Jesus being a guilt offering relates that the Servant would be blessed above all because He so loved the world that He willingly and *voluntarily poured out Himself* when He died for the sins of the people. He was humble enough to let others consider Him to be a sinner, when in fact He was without sin and bore their sins:

> Therefore, I will allot Him a portion with the great, and He will divide the booty with the strong; because *He poured out Himself* to death, and was numbered with the *transgressors;* yet He Himself *bore the sin of many* and interceded for the transgressors.
>
> —Isaiah 53:12

Was Jesus, some 750 years later, "numbered with the transgressors"? Did He intercede for those transgressors? The answers are yes and yes.

Matthew 27:38 describes the fulfillment of Isaiah 53:12 that He would be "numbered with the transgressors":

> At that time *two robbers* were crucified with Him, one on the right and one on the left.

Jesus Would Intercede for One of the Transgressors as Prophesied in Isaiah 53:12

Luke 23:39-43 fulfills the prophecy that He would intercede for the transgressors:

> And one of the criminals who were hanged there was hurling abuse at Him, saying, "Are You not the Christ? Save Yourself and us!"
>
> But the other answered, and rebuking him said, "Do you not even fear God, since you are under the same sentence of condemnation?
>
> "And we indeed justly, for we are receiving what we deserve for our deeds; but this man has done nothing wrong."
>
> And he was saying, "Jesus, remember me when You come in Your kingdom!"
>
> And He said to him, *"Truly I say to you, today you shall be with Me in Paradise."*

Arguments by Antagonists That Isaiah 52:13-53:12 Does Not Refer to the Messiah But Rather to the Jewish People

Antagonists argue that the Isaiah passage concerns the Jewish people and not the Messiah. Until approximately 1100 A.D., there was agreement among Jewish scholars and rabbis that Isaiah 52:13 through 53:12 referred to the Messiah. Antagonists of Christ must explain away this prophecy as not being Messianic. To accomplish this after 1100 A.D., the majority of Jewish scholars and rabbis changed and took the position that this prophecy did not speak of a specific person but, rather, the Jewish people. However, Jewish scholars and rabbis before and some even after 1100 A.D., admitted that Isaiah was speaking of the Messiah.

The following quotations are from *Jesus Was a Jew* by Dr. Arnold Fruchtenbaum, as we continue:

Isaiah Passages Refer to the Singular Messiah and Not the Jewish People, According to Most Rabbis

Rabbi Abarbanel, around 1500 A.D., while taking the position that the Isaiah passage did not refer to the Messiah, admits prior "learned men" concluded Isaiah was speaking of the Messiah:

> The first question is to ascertain to whom this prophecy refers, for the *learned among the Nazarenes* expound it of the man who *was crucified in Jerusalem* at the end of the Second Temple, and, who according to them, was the Son of God and took flesh in the *virgin's womb*, as is stated in their writings. Jonathan ben Uzziel interprets it in the Targum of the future Messiah; and this is *also* the opinion of our *learned men in the majority of their Midrashim*.

The Jewish Babylonian Talmud also took the Isaiah passage to refer to the Messiah, and Isaiah 53:4 specifically being applied to the person of the Messiah Himself. The view that this Isaiah passage speaks of the Messiah still predominated in the 10th century as seen from the commentary of Yepheth ben All:

> As for myself I am inclined with Benjamin of Nehavend to regard it as alluding to the Messiah . . . He [the prophet] thus gives us to understand two things: in the first instance, that the Messiah will only reach His highest degree of honor after long and severe trials; and secondly, that these trials will be sent upon Him as a kind of a sign, so that, if He finds Himself under the yoke of misfortunes while remaining pious in His actions He may know that He is the designated one . . . The expression "my servant" is applied *to the Messiah* as it is applied to his ancestor in the verse, I have sworn to David my servant.

The rabbis in the 11th century continued to consider the suffering servant described by Isaiah to speak of the Messiah. In *Bereshith Rabbah* by Rabbi Moshe Hadarshan, he writes:

> The Holy One gave *Messiah* the opportunity to save souls but to be severely chastised: and forth-

> with the *Messiah* accepted the chastisements of love, as it is written, He was oppressed and He was afflicted. And when Israel is sinful, the *Messiah* seeks mercy upon them; as it is written, by His stripes we are healed, and He carried the sins of many and made intercession for the transgressors.

Among the most famous rabbis of the 11th century was Moses ben Maimon, better known as Maimonides. He also states the Isaiah passage refers to the Messiah:

> Regarding the mission by which *Messiah* will present Himself . . . He will not commend Himself to our veneration by reason of His notable extraction; but the marvelous deeds He shall perform will show Him to be the anticipated Messiah . . . Isaiah states He grew like a tender plant and is a root out of dry ground, signifying that His descent will not be known till His successful career will direct people's attention to it . . . but a noteworthy circumstance will be that crowned heads will stand amazed . . . so they will remain in utter silence, as Isaiah predicts, at Him will kings shut their mouths, for what had not been told unto them shall they see, and what they never heard shall they understand.

Rabbi Moshe Kohen Ibn Crispin of Spain stated in 1350:

> I am pleased to interpret it in accordance of our rabbis, of the *King Messiah*, and will be careful, so far as I am able, to adhere to the literal sense: thus, possibly, I shall be free from the fancied and far-fetched interpretations of which others have been guilty.

As late as 1500 we have the words of Rabbi Saadhey Ibn

Danan of Granada:

> One of these words, Rabbi Joseph ben Kaspi, was led so far as to say that those who expounded it of the Messiah, who is shortly to be revealed, gave occasion to the heretics to interpret it of Jesus. May God, however, forgive him for not having spoken the truth! Our rabbis, the doctors of the Talmud, delivered their opinions by the power of prophecy, possess a tradition concerning the principles of interpretation . . . *alludes solely to the King Messiah*.

As Dr. Fruchtenbaum pointed out, to interpret Isaiah 53 as speaking of the Messiah is not non-Jewish. In fact, if we are to speak of the original traditional Jewish interpretation, it would be that the passage speaks of the Messiah. History reveals that the first rabbi to expound the view that this referred to Israel rather than the Messiah was Rabbi Rashi around 1105 A.D. But this view was contrary to all rabbinical teaching of that day and of the preceding 1,000 years.

The Search for Messiah by Eastman and Smith contains the following compelling quotations:

> Two centuries later we find the comments of another member of the Midrashim, Rabbi Elijah De Vidas, a Cabalistic scholar in the 16th century. In his comments of Isaiah 53 we read: The meaning of "He was wounded for our transgressions, bruised for our iniquities" is that since the Messiah bears our iniquities, which produce the effect of His being bruised, it follows that who will not admit that the *Messiah* thus suffers for our iniquities must endure and suffer them for himself.

We have also the writings of the 16th century Rabbi Moshe

el Sheikh, who declares in his work *Commentaries of the Earlier Prophets*, regarding the suffering servant in Isaiah 53:

> Our rabbis with one voice affirm the opinion that the prophet is speaking of the *King Messiah*, and we shall ourselves also adhere to the same view.

The text of Isaiah itself provides a number of compelling proofs as to what Isaiah meant. It is clear when reference is made to the individual Messiah, and it is equally clear when reference is made to the collective body of Israel. Again, Dr. Fruchtenbaum developed the following argument:

> Important proof as to whom this passage referred is the consistent use of pronouns. A distinction is made between the plural "we," "us," and "our" and the singular "He," "Him," and "His." Consistently the use of "we," "us," and "our" in the passage must refer collectively to Isaiah the prophet together with the Jewish people to whom Isaiah was speaking. The singular use of "He," "Him," and "His" must refer to the suffering servant.

The following passage in Isaiah makes this apparent:

> Surely *our* griefs *He* Himself bore, and *our* sorrows *He* carried; yet *we* ourselves esteemed *Him* stricken. Smitten of God, and afflicted.
>
> But *He* was pierced through for *our* transgressions, *He* was crushed for *our* iniquities; the chastening for *our* well-being fell upon *Him*, and by *His* scourging *we* are healed.
>
> All of *us* like sheep have gone astray, each of *us* has turned to *his* own way; but the Lord has caused the iniquity of *us* all to fall on *Him*.

> *He* was oppressed and *He* was afflicted, yet *He* did not open *His* mouth; like a lamb that is led to slaughter, and like a sheep that is silent before its shearers, so *He* did not open *His* mouth.
>
> By oppression and judgment *He* was taken away; and as for *His* generation, who considered that *He* was cut off out of the land of the living, for the transgression of *my people* to whom the stroke was due?
>
> *His* grave was assigned with wicked men, yet *He* was with a rich man in *His* death, because *He* had done no violence, nor was there any deceit in *His* mouth.
>
> —Isaiah 53:4-9

Thus, the first area of proof in the above passage that this prophecy does not speak only of the Jewish people is that the plural use of the pronouns "we," "us," and "our" refer to the Jewish people, including Isaiah. Isaiah is thus speaking to the Jewish people as a whole. He includes himself with the Jewish people. However, Isaiah represents the Messiah or the suffering servant in a different category by using the *singular* and personal pronouns "He," "*Him*," and "*His*." He is the one who is suffering for us. He is the one God on whom we lay our sins. He is the one who will die for *our* sins so that we can have salvation through *Him*. The constant and consistent use of these plural pronouns exclude the suffering servant from being Israel. Rather, the suffering servant is the Messiah, Himself.

The second area of proof is in the closing sentence of verse 8, which also serves to exclude Israel from being the suffering servant:

> . . . *He* was cut off out of the land of the living for the transgression of *my people* to whom the stroke was due.

As Isaiah views the death of the suffering servant, it was for the sins of "my people." No one questions Isaiah's people as being the Jews. And if "my people" are the Jews, they cannot be at the same time the singular suffering servant because in the same sentence, distinction is made between "He" and "my people." Hence, the suffering servant must refer to the individual Messiah.

The third proof is that throughout the entire passage the suffering servant is portrayed as a *singular* human personality.

The fourth proof is that the suffering servant is presented in the verses as an innocent sufferer. It is easy to see how this can be true of the Messiah, but it is impossible for the innocent sufferer to apply to the Jewish people or, for that matter, any people, because none are innocent. The prophet Isaiah never told the Jews that they would suffer for being innocent, but rather that they would suffer for their sins. God punished Israel many times and in various ways, and it was always for their sins and not because they were innocent.

The fifth proof is the suffering servant being portrayed as a voluntary, willing and silent sufferer. He willingly submits to the suffering He undergoes and voices no complaint as to the injustice being suffered. The Jewish people throughout biblical history could not be accused of being silent (see Numbers 11:1, 14:2-3, 14:27, and 16:13-14).

The sixth proof is the passage describing the Messiah suffering a vicarious and substitutionary death. He suffers for the sake of others, both Jews and Gentiles, so that they need not suffer for their sins. Nowhere in the Scriptures or in Jewish history do we ever see Israel suffering for Gentiles.

The seventh proof is crucial. According to Isaiah, the suffering servant dies and, of course, the Jewish people are alive.

Psalm 22:16-18

> A band of evildoers has encompassed me; they pierced my hands and my feet. I can count all my

> bones. They look, they stare at me; they divide my garments among them, and for my clothing they cast lots.
>
> —Psalm 22:16-18

This passage can be recited to virtually any person on earth, and they will conclude it speaks of the crucifixion of Jesus. Amazingly, it is from a Psalm written by King David a thousand years before the birth of Jesus! At the time King David made this prophecy, the Jews had never heard of death by crucifixion. The means of enforcing capital punishment by the Jews was *stoning*. This was true in both the Hebrew Scriptures (Leviticus 20:2) and the New Testament (Acts 7:59). In order for this prophecy to be fulfilled, some country that utilized death by crucifixion would have to conquer Israel. This was fulfilled in approximately 40 B.C. when Rome, which did use crucifixion, conquered Israel. Thus, this prophecy was historically in a position to be fulfilled by Jesus.

One Thousand Years Before the Crucifixion, David Prophesied What Would Physiologically Happen to Jesus When Crucified

King David, in the same Psalm that discusses the same person who was pierced, prophesies about this crucified Messiah in verses 14 and 15:

> I am poured out like water, and all *my bones are out of joint;* my *heart* is like *wax;* it is *melted* within me. My *strength is dried* up like a potsherd, and my *tongue cleaves to my jaws;* and Thou dost lay me in the dust of death.

This prophecy sets forth what would *physiologically* happen to the Messiah when He is being pierced and crucified:

1. He will be "poured out like water."
2. All His bones will be "out of joint."
3. His heart will turn to a substance like "wax" and will

be "melted" within Him.

4. His "strength" while dying will become "dried up like a potsherd" (cow chip).

5. His tongue "cleaves" to His jaws during His death.

The question arises as to whether or not all or any of the above physiological conditions are experienced by a person who suffers death by crucifixion such as Jesus. Let's take a closer look at these conditions.

"I am poured out like water" and "my heart is like wax; it is melted within me."

In order to determine physiologically the cause of death when a person is crucified, Dr. Samuel Houghton of the University of Dublin conducted a series of experiments. Dr. Houghton, as a result of these experiments, concluded that when a person is crucified, he often dies from a ruptured heart. When he dies from a *ruptured heart*, the pericardial sac that surrounds the heart bursts and, if the crucified person is pierced in the side, one can observe *blood followed by water* coming from this wound. Dr. Houghton thus established that this prophecy, which states that the person being crucified would be "poured out like water" and that his heart would be "like wax" and would be "melted within" him, is physiologically sound with death being caused by a ruptured heart.

An eyewitness at the foot of the cross of Jesus, before knowing of Dr. Houghton's experiments, confirmed this prophecy when he observed the side of Jesus being pierced and out came *blood followed by water*. That witness was the apostle John:

> But coming to Jesus, when they saw that He was already dead, they did not break His legs; but one of the soldiers *pierced* His side with a spear, and immediately there came out *blood and water*. And he who

> has seen has borne witness, and his witness is true; and he knows that he is telling the truth, so that you also may believe.
>
> —John 19:33-35

John was not a graduate pathologist from the University of Jerusalem but, rather, a fisherman describing his observations. The only thing that he knew was that when he was standing at the foot of the cross of Jesus, a spear went into His side and blood and then water flowed from this wound.

Dr. Houghton confirmed why this observation is so strikingly convincing as to the truth of Jesus' crucifixion and John's eyewitness testimony.

". . . and all my bones are out of joint."

The next physiological condition prophesied to be experienced by the Messiah when He was crucified was that all of His bones would be "out of joint." This has been confirmed by observations that when a person is hanging from a cross, the force of gravity pulls his joints apart so that they are in fact "out of joint."

"My strength is dried up like a potsherd . . ."

The Messiah, when being pierced and crucified it was prophesied, would experience His "strength" being "dried up like a potsherd" or dried cow dung. When a person is crucified, this again is precisely what happens. Thus, this prophecy was yet again fulfilled by Jesus on the cross.

". . . and my tongue cleaves to my jaws."

Thus it was prophesied that the tongue of the Messiah, when being crucified, "cleaves" to His jaws. A person being crucified experiences such extreme thirst that his tongue "cleaves" to his jaws.

"I can count all my bones."

Psalm 22:17 says, "I *can count* all my bones." This psalm also prophesied that when the Messiah would be crucified and look to the ground, His bones would be out of joint and could be observed and counted. This was fulfilled by Jesus because anyone being crucified experiences gravity pulling apart such bones. Jesus, because of this, knew His bones were "out of joint" and could count them when looking down from the Cross.

Other Prophecies Set Forth in Psalm 22

"They divide my garments, and for my clothing they cast lots."

Psalm 22:18 prophesied, "They *divide* my garments among them, and for my clothing they *cast lots*." Thus it was prophesied that not only would His garments be divided, but this division would be determined by casting lots. This prophecy was fulfilled not by Jesus' disciples or others who believed in Him but by pagan Roman soldiers. This fulfillment is recorded in Matthew 27:35: "And when they had crucified Him, they divided up His garments among themselves, *casting lots*." The fulfillment of this prophecy was when they did not tear but divided His garments. This was accomplished by "casting lots." Jewish garments rendered themselves to being easily divided since they consisted separately of a headdress and inner and outer garments.

"My God, my God, why hast Thou forsaken me?"

Psalm 22:1 states: "My God, my God, why hast Thou forsaken me?" These identical words were uttered by Jesus from the cross in Matthew 27:46:

"And about the ninth hour Jesus cried out with a

> loud voice saying, 'Eli, Eli, Lama Sabachthani?' That is, 'My God, my God, why hast Thou forsaken Me?' "

Jesus recited the exact words of Psalm 22, saying undoubtedly that Psalm 22 speaks of Him.

"All who see Me, sneer at Me."

Psalm 22:7-8 prophesies that the Messiah, from the Cross, would observe that "All who see Me, sneer at Me" and "they wag the head":

> All who see Me, *sneer* at Me; they separate with the lip, they *wag* the head, saying, "Commit yourself to the Lord; let Him deliver Him; let Him rescue Him, because He delights in Him."

The fulfillment of this prophecy is recorded in Mark 15:29-30:

> And those passing by were hurling *abuse* at Him, *wagging* their heads, and saying, "Ha! You who are going to destroy the temple and rebuild it in three days, save Yourself and come down from the cross."

And again in Luke 23:35:

> And the people stood by, looking on, and even the rulers were *sneering* at Him, saying, "He saved others; let Him save Himself if this is the Christ of God, His Chosen One."

"He keeps all His bones, not one of them is broken."

Psalm 34:20 prophetically states what John observed some 1,000 years later—that Jesus' legs would not be broken: "He keeps all His bones, not one of them is broken." If the Roman soldiers had broken Jesus' legs, He would have been disqualified from being the Messiah because the Messiah must have fulfilled *all* of these prophecies, not just some of them. John 19:33 describes the fulfillment of this prophecy.

The Road to Emmaus—Luke 24:13-35

Two disciples (not apostles) on the road to Emmaus, immediately after the Crucifixion and Resurrection, were discussing these events when the resurrected Jesus Christ came upon them. "Their eyes were prevented from recognizing Him," Scripture says. Jesus feigned not knowing what they were talking about (Luke 24:17). The men were astonished at His ignorance of these well-known events. Even though there were undoubtedly scars on His body, Jesus used the most persuasive evidence—Messianic prophecies—to explain who He was:

> And beginning with Moses and with all the prophets, He explained to them the things concerning Himself in all the Scriptures.
>
> —Luke 24:27

What was the effect of Jesus Christ explaining these Messianic prophecies?

> And they said to one another, "Were not our hearts burning within us while He was speaking to us on the road, while He was explaining the Scriptures to us?"
>
> —Luke 24:32

A more illustrative and profound lesson by Jesus Christ regarding the use of prophecies to explain who He is would not be comprehensible. Can we believers do any less?

Mathematical Probability of Fulfillment by Chance of the Messianic Prophecies

There are over 300 prophecies concerning the Messiah that were fulfilled and could only be fulfilled by the life of Jesus. Someone calculated the mathematical probability of a person fulfilling by chance just eight of the 300 prophecies. The conclusion was that there was one chance in 10^{17}. So that we can understand the enormity of this number, if silver dollars two feet high covered the entire state of Texas, and only one was made in 1989, the mathematical probability of a person selecting that single 1989 silver dollar would be 10^{17}. In other words, impossible.

What is the reason for God outlining in such detail the prophecies concerning His Son and their fulfillment? That question is answered in John 20:31:

> "But these have been written that you may believe that Jesus is the Christ, the Son of God; and that believing you may have life in His name."

Jesus verified that all things written about him in the Law of Moses, the prophets, and the Psalms must be fulfilled:

> Now He said to them, "These are My words which I spoke to you while I was still with you, that all things which are written *about* Me in the *Law* of Moses and the *Prophets* and the *Psalms must be fulfilled.*" Then He opened their minds to understand the Scriptures.
>
> —Luke 24:44-45

Finally, after years of irrational arguments made by antagonists of Christ, the admission is made that the historicity of Christ is beyond dispute and fulfills a prominent part of the historical scene. In fact, they also must admit that no one matches this prominence as a historical figure. Chapter 7 develops this theme.

The Historicity of Jesus the Messiah

7

Even the historicity of Jesus, out of frustration, has been questioned. However, the *Encyclopedia Britannica* (volume 10, page 145) puts this argument to rest:

> In the Talmud, a compendium of Jewish law, lore and commentary, only a few statements of the rabbis (Jewish religious teachers) of the first and second centuries come into consideration. Containing mostly polemics or Jewish apologetics, they reveal an acquaintance with the Christian tradition but include several divergent legendary motifs as well. The *picture of Jesus* offered in these writings may be summarized as follows: born as the illegitimate son of a Roman soldier called Panther, Jesus (Hebrew Yeshua) worked magic, ridiculed the wise, seduced and stirred up the people, gathered five disciples about him, and was *hanged* (crucified) *on the eve of the Passover*. These independent accounts prove that in ancient times even the

> opponents of Christianity never doubted the historicity of Jesus, which was disputed for the first time and on inadequate grounds by several authors at the end of the 18th, during the 19th, and at the beginning of the 20th centuries.

The above quotation from the *Encyclopedia Britannica* establishes not only the historicity of Jesus, but the historicity of His Crucifixion. The Jewish Talmud also in this quotation acknowledges the historicity of Jesus' crucifixion "on the eve of Passover."

Antiquities by the Jewish historian Josephus at 20:9 has this detailed account of Christ and His blood brother, James, establishing Christ's historicity:

> After the death of the procurator Festus, when Albinus was about to succeed him, the high priest Ananius considered it a favorable opportunity to assemble the Sanhedrin. He therefore caused *James, the brother of Jesus* who was called *Christ*, and several others, to appear before this hastily assembled council. The wise men and strict observers of the law who were at Jerusalem expressed their disapprobation of this act . . . some even went to Albinus himself, who had departed to Alexandria, to bring this breach of the law under his observation, and to inform him that Ananius had acted illegally in assembling the Sanhedrin without the Roman authority.

Again in *Antiquities* 18:33:

> Now there was about this time *Jesus*, a wise man, if it be lawful to call Him a man; for He

> was a doer of wonderful works, a teacher of such men as receive the *truth* with pleasure. He drew over to Him many Jews, and also many of the Greeks. This man *was the* Christ. And when Pilate had condemned Him to the cross, upon His impeachment by the principal man among us, those who had loved Him from the first did not forsake Him, for He appeared to them *alive* on the third day, the divine prophets having spoken these and thousands of other wonderful things about Him. And even now, the race of Christians, so named from Him, has not died out.

Many other non-biblical historians refer to the life, death, and resurrection of Jesus Christ, such as the following: Roman historians Cornelius Tacitus, Seutonius, Plinius Secundus, and Justin Martyr; Samaritan historian Thallius; and Syrian Mara Bar-Serapion, as well as the above indicated Jewish Talmud, which refers to Jesus as "Ben Pandera."

Oh, how many times have I heard the argument that not even Jesus or the Bible claims that Jesus is God? Chapter 8 puts to rest such a futile argument. Not only does Jesus and the Bible clearly establish Jesus' deity, but also that Jesus Christ has existed eternally and with no beginning and no end.

Jesus the Messiah Is Described as God

8

Isaiah described the child that was to be born as "Mighty God" in Isaiah 9:6:

> For a child will be born to us, a son will be given to us; and the government will rest on His shoulders; and His name will be called Wonderful, Counselor, *Mighty God*, Eternal Father, Prince of Peace.

"The Angel of the Lord" who was seen on over twelve occasions in the Hebrew Scriptures, was identified as the Messiah, God, or Lord. (See page 88 for this evidence.) The author of Judges in the Hebrew Scriptures was probably Samuel, who explained that the name of "The Angel of the Lord" was "Wonderful," the same name used in Isaiah 9:6 to describe Jesus.

> But the Angel of the Lord said to him, why do you ask my name since it is *Wonderful?*
>
> —Judges 13:18

The Hebrew Scriptures reveal that God the Son as the second member of the Trinity has existed eternally, including the time encompassed in the Hebrew Scriptures. The Jewish prophet Micah prophesied 700 years before the birth of Jesus that He would be born in Bethlehem. Micah explained that although Jesus became incarnate (taking on human form), He had existed "from the days of eternity":

> But as for you, Bethlehem Ephrathah, too little to be among the clans of Judah, from you One will go forth from Me to be ruler of Israel. His goings forth are from long ago, *from the days of eternity.*
>
> —Micah 5:2

Who was it that was to be born in Bethlehem? Micah answers this question by explaining that the one being born had existed "from the days of eternity." Clearly no one but God has existed eternally. This, therefore, is a prophesy by a Jewish prophet that God Himself would be born in Bethlehem.

Isaiah explained that the child who was to be born of a virgin would be called "Immanuel," which means "God with us":

> Therefore the Lord Himself will give you a sign: Behold a virgin will be with child and bare a son, and she will call his name *Immanuel.*
>
> —Isaiah 7:14

King David in the Psalms describes God the Father installing "My King" upon Mount Zion and establishing King Messiah as "My Son":

> But as for Me, I have installed My *King* Upon Zion, my holy mountain. I will surely tell of the decree of the Lord: He said to Me, Thou art My Son, today I have begotten Thee.
>
> —Psalm 2:6-7

Jewish theology teaches that the "Son of God" *is God*. Jesus said in many places that He is the Son of God:

> Again, the high priest was questioning Him and saying to Him are you the Christ, the Son of the Blessed One? And Jesus said, "*I am.*"
>
> —Mark 14:61b, 62a

When Jesus used the term "I am," the high priest understood that Jesus claimed to be God because in Mark 14:64, he said Jesus committed blasphemy for using that term. God in Exodus 3:14 refers to Himself as "I am."

> And they all said, "Are You the Son of God, then?" And He said to them, "Yes, *I am.*"
>
> —Luke 22:70

The Bible states in other places that Jesus Christ, the second member of the Trinity, was and is God. This is brought out in the Book of Titus:

> Looking at the blessed hope and the appearing of the glory of our *great God and Savior, Jesus Christ.*
>
> —Titus 2:13

> But when the kindness of *God our Savior* and His love for mankind appeared He saved us not on the basis of deeds which we have done in righteousness but according to His mercy by the washing of regeneration and renewing by the Holy Spirit whom he poured out upon us richly through *Jesus Christ our Savior.*
>
> —Titus 3:4-6

Also, 2 Peter 1:1:

> Simon Peter, a bondservant and apostle of Jesus Christ, to those who have received a faith of the same kind as ours, by the righteousness of our *God* and Savior, Jesus Christ.

Thus, the conclusion of the teaching in the Hebrew Scriptures and the New Testament is that Jesus the Messiah was and is the true God. The Hebrew Scriptures and Jesus give us no alternative: Jesus was either a liar and a lunatic, or He was Lord.

How important is our belief that Jesus is Lord? Eternity is determined by our answer:

> If you confess with your mouth Jesus is Lord... you will be saved.
>
> —Romans 10:9

If the Bible sets forth the lineage of Jesus hundreds of years before His birth (and it does just that), with no studies even attempting to refute that lineage, would that be persuasive as to Him being the Messiah? If such lineage was available in the temple records for any of Jesus' antagonists to determine if such prophecies were accurate—and no one did—would that be persuasive as to Him being the Messiah? The prophecies of Jesus' ancestors, made centuries before His birth, is the subject of Chapter 9.

Credentials and Lineage of Jesus the Messiah, as Prophesied 9

The biblical *credentials* and *lineage* of Jesus the Messiah setting forth His forefathers 700 to 1,400 years before His birth are found in the following prophecies of the Hebrew Scriptures:

1. Jesus the Messiah will be Jewish and come through *only* the seed of *Abraham* (Genesis 22:18).

2. Abraham had eight sons, including Isaac and Ishmael, and Jesus the Messiah was prophesied to come *only* through *Isaac* (Genesis 26:4).

3. Isaac had two sons, Jacob and Esau, and it was prophesied that Jesus the Messiah must come through *only Jacob* (Genesis 28:14).

4. Jacob had twelve sons, from whom came the twelve tribes of Israel, and it was prophesied that Jesus the Messiah must come through *only* the *tribe of Judah* (Genesis 49:10).

5. Of the thousands of families in the tribe of Judah, it was prophesied that Jesus the Messiah must come through only the family of *Jesse* (Isaiah 11:1-2).

6. Jesse had eight sons, and it was prophesied that Jesus the

Messiah must come through *only* Jesse's youngest son, *David* (Psalm 132:11).

In Matthew 1:1-17 the genealogy of Jesus Christ, *through Joseph*, His supposed father, is set forth through the following forty ancestors: Abraham, Isaac, Jacob, Judah, Perez, Hezron, Ram, Amminadab, Nahchon, Salmon, Boaz, Obed, Jesse, David, *Solomon*, Rehoboam, Abijah, Assa, Jehoshaphat, Joram, Uzziah, Jotham, Ahaz, Hezekiah, Manasseh, Amon, Josiah, *Jeconiah*, Shealtiel, Zerubbabel, Abiud, Eliakim, Azor, Zadok, Achim, Eliud, Eleazar, Matthan, Jacob, and Joseph.

The genealogy of Jesus Christ, *through Mary*, His mother is set forth through the following seventy-two ancestors in Luke 3:23-38: Matthat, Melchi, Jannai, Joseph, Mattathias, Amos, Nahum, Hesli, Naggai, Maath, Mattathias, Semein, Josech, Joda, Joanan, Rhesa, Zerubbabel, Shealtiel, Neri, Melchi, Addi, Cosam, Elmadam, Er, Joshua, Eliezer, Jorim, Matthat, Levi, Simeon, Joseph, Jonam, Eliakim, Melea, Menna, Mattatha, *Nathan*, *David*, Jesse, Boaz, Salmon, Nahshon, Amminadab, Admin, Ram, Hezron, Perez, Juda, Jacob, Isaac, Abraham, Terah, Nahor, Serug, Reu, Peleg, Heber, Shelah, Cainan, Arphaxad, Shem, Noah, Lamech, Methuselah, Enoch, Jared, Mahalaleel, Cainan, Enos, Neosh, Seth, and Adam.

Jeremiah 22:24-30 explains in reference to Coniah, a.k.a. Jeconiah, that "For no man of his descendants will prosper, sitting on the throne of David, or ruling again in Judah" (verse 30). Thus, God commands that none of the descendants of Jeconiah shall sit on the throne of David. Yet, Matthew 1:11 says Joseph descended through Jeconiah. If therefore the blood of Joseph was in Jesus, He would be *precluded* from being the Messiah. Did Jesus have Joseph's blood? The answer is no because Mary was a virgin (Isaiah 7:14) and became pregnant through the Holy Spirit (Luke 1:35) and not by Joseph.

Was Mary descended from Jeconiah, which would disqualify Jesus from being the Messiah? Of course, the blood of Mary was in Jesus, and therefore the answer to this question is pivotal. If Mary descended from Jeconiah, Jesus could not be the Messiah! The answer is no because Mary descended from David's son, Nathan, and not Solomon (Luke 3:31). Jeconiah descended only through David's son, Solomon, and not Nathan (Matthew 1:6). That is why Jeconiah is only mentioned in the lineage of Joseph (Matthew 1:11) and not Mary. Can you think of any evidence more compelling and exacting, pointing only to Jesus as having the requisite lineage? I cannot.

What is the point of the Bible prophesying about Jesus' ancestors? Answer: so that we can know the truth that Jesus the Son of God *is* the Messiah. Until the destruction of the Jewish temple in 70 A.D., the genealogy of not only Jesus but of each of His ancestors was available in the temple for anyone to study.

Contained in the Jewish second temple, which was destroyed in 70 A.D. by the Romans, were the genealogical records of all of the Jews dating back to the time of Abraham. 1 Chronicles 9:1 establishes the keeping of these genealogical records:

> So all Israel was enrolled by genealogies; and behold, they are written in the Book of the Kings of Israel.

Jesus Christ claimed that He alone fulfilled the prophecies set forth in the Hebrew Scriptures. Jesus explained this in Matthew 5:17-18:

> "Do not think that I came to abolish the Law or the Prophets; I did not come to abolish, *but to fulfill*. For truly I say to you, until heaven and earth pass away, not the smallest letter or stroke shall pass away from the Law, until all is accomplished."

It was well known to the Jewish people that Jesus Christ claimed to be *the son of David* and, therefore, His lineage was from King David (see Matthew 9:27, 12:22-23, and 15:22). Specifically, the Pharisees knew of the claims of Jesus that He fulfilled these prophecies as observed in Matthew 22:41-46:

> Now while the Pharisees were gathered together, Jesus asked them a question, saying, "What do you think about the Christ, whose son is He?" They said to Him, *"The son of David."* He said to them, "Then how does David in the Spirit call Him Lord, saying, 'The Lord said to my Lord, sit at my right hand, until I put thine enemies beneath thy feet?' If David then calls Him Lord, how is He his son?" No one was able to answer Him a word, nor did anyone dare from that day on to ask Him another question.

King David's lineage, as well as that of Abraham, Isaac, Jacob, Judah and Jesse, were recorded in the second temple and could easily be traced and compared to lineage of Jesus the Messiah, which was also recorded in the second temple. The lineage of Mary and Joseph was available as well. His enemies must have done this, as they did everything else they could think of to refute His Messiahship.

At the time of Jesus Christ's ministry, He had precious few followers (Isaiah 53:1). There was an attempt at every turn to discredit Him. At no time, however, did anyone contest His credentials or lineage. At no time did any antagonist attempt to refute the genealogy of Jesus the Messiah as prophesied in the Hebrew Scriptures. It would have been a simple matter for anyone to go to the historical records contained in the second temple to prove that the genealogy of Jesus the Messiah did not come through Abraham, Isaac, Jacob, the tribe of Judah, the family of Jesse, and finally through David.

In the New Testament as well, the genealogy of Jesus was publicly proclaimed, for anyone to refute. Matthew 1:1-17 set forth the lineage of Jesus through Joseph, and Luke 3:23-38 set forth the lineage of Jesus through Mary, which, if false, could be challenged through the same second temple records.

Thus, it is historically unchallenged that the genealogy set forth of Jesus Christ in the Hebrew Scriptures and in the New Testament could only have been fulfilled by Jesus Christ.

Just as my residence at 895 Panorama Road, Palm Springs, California, USA, eliminates all other possible residences in the world, the genealogy of Jesus as set forth in the Hebrew Scriptures and Luke eliminates all other Jews or Gentiles except for Jesus being the Messiah, because only Jesus had these precise ancestors. (The Bible divides the entire world population into Jews and Gentiles.) The fact that my residence is in the USA eliminates all other countries, the fact that it is in California eliminates all other states, the fact that it is in Palm Springs eliminates all other cities, the fact that it is on Panorama Road eliminates all other roads, and the fact that it has a street number of 895 eliminates all other residences on that road.

Looking Ahead

Why is there an attempt by some to deny the Jewishness of Jesus? Because if Jesus' Jewish ancestry can be discredited, then any or all of the Old Testament prophecies pointing to Him as the Jewish Messiah can be discredited as well. Yet Jesus was Jewish (all of Jesus' ancestors were Jewish, save for three Gentile women). Jesus said He came to fulfill everything in the Old Testament. Everything! Of all the peoples in the world, the Jews should welcome Jesus with open arms as one of their own. I will discuss why in the next chapter.

70 • Verdict: Jesus Christ Is Who He Said He Was

Of All People, the Jews Should Be Most Comfortable in the Presence of Christ

God the Son, who was described in the *Hebrew Scriptures* as existing eternally, became God incarnate when He assumed an earthly body upon His birth in Bethlehem. All of the ancestors of Jesus were Jewish, beginning with Abraham and ending with Mary, with the exception of three Gentile women two of which were guilty of sexual promiscuity (Matthew 1:5-6).

Jesus during His earthly ministry prohibited His disciples from going to the Gentiles, but rather only to "the house of Israel" in Matthew 10:5-6:

> These twelve Jesus sent out after instructing them, saying, "Do not go in the way of the Gentiles, and do not enter any city of the Samaritans; but rather go to the lost sheep of the *house of Israel*."

Jesus again confirmed that His ministry on earth was confined to the Jewish people in Matthew 15:24: "I was sent only to the lost sheep of the house of Israel."

All forty authors of the Bible were Jewish, with the possible exception of Luke. All of the apostles of Jesus Christ were Jewish.

The first Christian martyr, Stephen, was Jewish. The first leader of the Christian church in Jerusalem was James of the tribe of Judah, also the half-brother of Jesus.

Did our Lord, when He worshiped, go to some New Testament church that was built in competition with the synagogues? No, indeed; when Jesus worshiped, He worshiped at the synagogues:

> And He came to Nazareth, where He had been brought up, and as was His custom, He entered the *synagogue* on the Sabbath, and stood up to read.
>
> —Luke 4:16

Jesus referred to the temple in Jerusalem as "My Father's house" and "My house":

> And He said to them, "Why is it that you were looking for Me? Did you not know that I had to be in My *Father's* house?"
>
> —Luke 2:49

> And He said to them, "It is written, My *house* shall be called a house of prayer; but you are making it a robbers' den."
>
> —Matthew 21:13

The First Believers in Jesus Were Forced Out of the Synagogues

For approximately 100 years after the crucifixion and resurrection of Jesus, Hebrew Christians were accepted as a sect of Judaism, not separate and apart from Judaism. History reveals that along with the Zealots, Essenes, Pharisees, and Sadducees, Hebrew Christians were so regarded. The Bible reveals that the apostles did not go to the temple in Jerusalem just to evangelize, but also to worship in Acts 3:1: "Now Peter and John were going up to the temple at the ninth hour, the hour of prayer."

The clear historical conclusion that many of the first believers in Jesus were Jewish, and at the same time "zealous for the law," is confirmed in Acts 21:20:

> And when they heard it they began glorifying God; and they said to him, "You see, brother, how many thousands there are among the Jews of those who have believed, and they are all *zealous* for the Law."

Therefore, the Bible teaches that Hebrew Christians, along with other Jews, worshiped at the Jerusalem temple and in the synagogues, and observed Jewish religious practices. The argument is often made that if Jesus really was the Messiah, Jewish people of His day would have accepted Him as such. As we have observed, the historical record reveals that to be precisely the case—that many Jewish people of His day *did* accept Him as the Messiah.

In view of the above truth, we must ask: What happened to separate Hebrew Christians from the other Jews? The following is revealed in the historical record and answers that question.

From 66 to 70 A.D., the first Jewish revolt against Rome occurred. The leader of the Hebrew Christians during this time was Simon, a cousin of James and Jesus. Hebrew Christians fought alongside other Jews in this revolt against Rome. During this revolt, the Roman army surrounded Jerusalem. Jesus told His followers when this occurred they were to flee to the mountains in Luke 21:20-21:

> "But when you see *Jerusalem surrounded by armies*, then recognize that her desolation is at

> hand. Then let those who are in Judea flee to the mountains, and let those who are in the midst of the city depart, and let not those who are in the country enter the city."

Because Hebrew Christians observed *Jerusalem surrounded by armies*, they had a dilemma—whether to follow God's instructions and flee to the mountains, or follow man's instructions and continue to fight alongside their fellow Jewish citizens. These Jewish Christians chose to follow Jesus' instructions and fled to the mountains of Bozrah, which is present-day Petra in Southern Jordan. When this occurred, these Hebrew Christians were labeled traitors. Shortly after they fled to the mountains, the prophecy of Jesus that Jerusalem and the temple would be destroyed occurred. Because of this fulfilled prophecy, many Jews accepted Jesus as their Savior and Messiah.

From 132 to 135 A.D., the second Jewish revolt against Rome occurred. The leader of this Jewish revolt was Bar Cochba. Having long since returned from Bozrah after the first Jewish revolt, Hebrew Christians again joined with their fellow Jews in fighting against Rome, until Rabbi Akiba declared that Bar Cochba was the Messiah. The Jewish leader Bar Cochba, being declared the Messiah, changed the second revolt against Rome from a political to a religious war. Hebrew Christians refused to acknowledge that Bar Cochba was the Messiah. This again forced them to withdraw from the Jewish community. A complete breakdown then resulted between other Jews and Hebrew Christians, who were labeled again as traitors. If anyone was to blame for turning Christianity into a so called Gentile religion, it was Bar Cochba and not Jesus. After this second Jewish revolt, Jerusalem was again destroyed.

Therefore, the conclusion of history is that Hebrew Christians did not leave the synagogue voluntarily, but rather were *forced out* by the leadership of that day.

The Apostle Paul on Anti-Semitism

Paul speaks directly to Gentile believers on the subject of anti-Semitism in Romans 11:13-18:

> But I am speaking to you who are Gentiles. Inasmuch then as I am an apostle of Gentiles, I magnify my ministry, if somehow I might move to jealousy my fellow countrymen and save some of them.
>
> For if their rejection be the reconciliation of the world, what will their acceptance be but life from the dead? And if the first piece of dough be holy, the lump is also; and if the root be holy, the branches are too.
>
> But if some of the branches were *broken off*, and you, being a wild olive, were grafted in among them and became partaker with them of the rich root of the olive tree, do not be arrogant toward the branches; but if you are arrogant, remember that it is not you who supports the root, but the root supports you.

In the above passage, "root" refers to Abraham and the prophets, "branches" refers to the Israeli people, "olive tree" refers to a Jewish place of blessing, and "wild olive" refers to Gentile believers. Therefore, the teaching of Paul was that Gentile believers are grafted into the Jewish olive tree and not vice-versa; and that Gentile believers should not become arrogant or scornful toward the Jewish people.

We, Gentiles, should realize that it was not God's divine plan to form a new religion superceding the Hebrew Scriptures. Gentiles receive their blessings through the Jews. We Gentiles should be on guard for all forms of anti-Semitism as being contrary to the teaching of the Bible. God's special relationship with the Jews, His chosen people, must be understood and followed to receive the blessings of Abraham and the other prophets. Finally, these blessings are available to believers only if they will carry out the mandate of Romans 1:16:

> For I am not ashamed of the gospel, for it is the power of God for salvation to every one who believes, to the *Jew first* and also to the Greek.

The Bible therefore teaches to Gentiles that blessings will come to them from the Jewish people. Thus not only does God's plan for Israel center around the Jews, but also God's plan for the Gentiles.

Satan Is the Source of All Anti-Semitism

Jesus told the Jews that He would not return until they, the Jews, pleaded for His return in Matthew 23:39:

> "For I say to you, from now on you shall not see Me until you say, 'Blessed is He who comes in the name of the Lord!' "

The phrase, "Blessed is He who comes in the name of the Lord" in Jewish theology refers only to a plea for the return of the Messiah. Thus, if there is no remnant of Jews to plead for His return, He will not return.

Who is a biblical scholar without peer? Satan, that's who (see Matthew 4:6). How could Satan avoid the second coming of Jesus? By *killing* all the Jews so that there would be no Jews to plead for His return.

Does history reflect this attempt to kill all the Jews? The answer to that question is well known by the entire world. This attempt began in Exodus 1:15-17 when the King of Egypt gave orders to kill all male Jewish babies, and continued in

Esther 3:13 when King Ahasuerus of Persia gave orders "to kill and annihilate all the Jews." This genocide continued after biblical times throughout the world, including the Spanish Inquisition in 1492, the 20th century Holocaust by Hitler and Nazi Germany, and more recently, militant Arabs and terrorist groups.

This attempt to kill all the Jews explains history that otherwise is inexplicable. There are racist feelings toward many minorities, but only the Jews experienced an attempt to eradicate them. Satan's attempted genocide will be unsuccessful. God promised that there will always be a remnant of Jews in Isaiah 66:22.

The clear conclusion of all this is that not only is anti-Semitism, in whatever form, satanic in origin, but also the attempted annihilation of the Jews.

God's Foreign Policy for Gentiles

The foreign policy for Gentiles is set forth in Genesis 12:3:

> "And I will *bless* those *who bless you*, and the one who *curses you* I will *curse*. And in you all the families of the earth shall be blessed."

Understanding this principle explains history that otherwise cannot be explained. God will bless those Gentiles that bless the Jews, and He will curse those Gentiles that curse the Jews. Biblical history confirms this:

1. The king of Egypt in Exodus 1:15-16 ordered the killing of all male Jewish *babies*. Thereafter, the last plague of God against Egypt, just before the Exodus, was likewise the killing of their firstborn. This was set forth in Exodus 12:29 and was a fulfillment of Genesis 12:3.

2. God promised in Exodus 17:8-16 to blot out the memory of Amalek because they fought against Israel, which

was fulfilled in 1 Samuel 15:1-9 when they were also destroyed. This was a fulfillment of Genesis 12:3.

3. Mordecai, a Jew, did not bow down to Haman, a Persian, in Esther 3:2. Haman had ordered all Jews to so do. Because of this defiance by Mordecai, genocide of the Jews was made a national policy of Persia by Haman (Esther 3:6). In Esther 5:13-14, the gallows that were built by Haman for Mordecai were instead used against him when the king ordered Haman to be hanged on the gallows intended for Mordecai (Esther 7:10). Again, this was a fulfillment of Genesis 12:3. Adolf Eichmann, who was instrumental in Nazi Germany for the extermination of millions of Jews, was reported to have said these last words just before he was hanged in 1947: "Haman 1947."

The secular historical record after biblical time reveals a continuing fulfillment of God, blessing those who bless the Jews and cursing those who do not:

1. The Spanish empire was powerful, and its armada controlled vast parts of the world. In 1492, an edict was made *expelling the Jews* from Spain. Shortly thereafter the Spanish armada was destroyed, and Spain's holdings in the Western Hemisphere were lost.

2. It was once said that the sun would never set on Great Britain, and not coincidentally, the Balfour Declaration during World War I established a home for the Jews. Thereafter, Great Britain won two world wars. In 1947, Great Britain would not allow the entrance of the Jews into Palestine. Thereafter, one possession after another of Great Britain was lost, the final ones being India and the Suez. Again, this was a fulfillment of Genesis 12:3. Ironically, both India and the Suez were obtained by Great Britain during the term of Prime Minister Disraeli, a Jew.

3. The Arab states of Syria, Iraq, Jordan, and Egypt in 1967 combined their forces in an attack on Israel. Nasser of Egypt said he would drive the Jews into the Mediterranean.

The opposite occurred, however, and the Egyptians retreated to the Suez. Hussein of Jordan said that Jordan would include all of Palestine. The opposite occurred, however, and he also retreated back to Jordan. During this war, Israel gained control of the old city of Jerusalem, previously under the control of Jordan. This is yet another example of the fulfillment of Genesis 12:3.

Indeed, most would say that Jesus Christ's life began in Bethlehem. Wrong! In fact, the life of Jesus Christ has no beginning. He was not created; rather He has lived eternally. If one thinks otherwise, he or she trivializes Jesus Christ's life. We will learn more about how the life of Christ did not begin in Bethlehem in Chapter 11.

The Life of Christ Did Not Begin in Bethlehem

Does our study of the life of Jesus Christ begin at Bethlehem? Do we at Christmas celebrate the birth of the Son of God? The answers are no and no. Okay, you say, when did it start? Answer: It did not. Rather, God the Son, along with God the Father and the Holy Spirit, have existed eternally. They have no beginning and no end.

The Trinity consisting of God the Father, God the Son, and God the Holy Spirit was described by Moses in the first chapter of the first book of the Jewish Bible:

> And the earth was formless and void and darkness was over the surface of the deep and the *spirit of God* was moving over the surface of the waters.
>
> —Genesis 1:2

> Then God said, "Let us make man in *our* image and according to *our* likeness. . . ."
>
> —Genesis 1:26

How do we know that Moses, the author of Genesis, was

referring to the Trinity in the above verses? Because God the Father was speaking to God the Son, saying let "us" make man in "our" image and according to "our" likeness in eternity past, prior to the creation of mankind. Only God has existed eternally. Therefore, "us" must refer to God the Father and God the Son. And in Genesis 1:2, the *Holy Spirit* was also identified in the same time frame as existing eternally.

We also see the same concept of "us" in Genesis 3:22:

> Then the Lord God, said Behold, "The man has become like one of *us*, knowing good and evil."

The "us" is referred to again in the famous Tower of Babel story:

> And the Lord said, "Behold, they are one people and they all have the same language. And this is what they began to do and now nothing which they purpose to do will be impossible for them. Come, let *Us* go down and there confuse their language, that they will not understand one another's speech."
>
> —Genesis 11:6-7

And finally, the concept of "us" is again seen in Isaiah 6:8:

> Then I heard the voice of the Lord saying, "Whom shall I send and who will go for *us?*"

What have we concluded about the existence and origin of Christ? He was not created but has existed eternally. He has no beginning and no end.

> And God created man in His own image and in the image of God He created a male and female.
>
> —Genesis 1:27

The time setting here is critical to understand; it was in eternity past. Man was not created in the image of the angels but in the image of God. To think that each of us has been made in the image of God is an awesome, mind-boggling concept. Our bodies are temples of God. We sinners, believers and unbelievers, were all made in the image of God. What a responsibility each of us has because of this heritage!

For further confirmation of Christ's eternal existence, see again Micah 5:2. Although I tried as an agnostic to find a loophole in this persuasive prophecy, I could not. This prophecy, made 750 years before Jesus' birth, stated that He would be born in Bethlehem and that He had existed "from the days of eternity":

> But as for you, Bethlehem Ephrathah, too little to be among the clans of Judah, from you one will go forth for me to be ruler in Israel, His goings forth are long ago from the days of *eternity*.

In this passage not only was Jesus' birth in Bethlehem prophesied 750 years before it occurred, but it explained that He had existed eternally. We are getting the picture, are we not, that the second member of the Godhead, Jesus Christ, has lived forever?

In Revelation 1:17 Jesus explains: "I am the first and the last," thus confirming His eternal existence. Because He was the Creator of everything, He has to have lived eternally. He has no beginning and no end:

> "Surely My hand *founded* the earth. And My right hand spread out the Heavens, when I call to them, they stand together. Assemble all of you and listen. Who among them has declared these things?"
>
> —Isaiah 48:13-14

Jesus Christ was speaking in the above passage and explaining that He founded the earth before the creation. Jesus again confirms

His eternal existence in John 17:24, explaining that God the Father loved Him "before the foundation of the world"—in other words, eternally.

John explained in John 1:1-3 that Jesus Christ was "the Word" and that He was "in the *beginning* with God," as we previously learned in Genesis 1:26:

> In the beginning was the Word, and the Word was with God, and the Word was God. He was in the beginning with God. All things came into being by Him, and apart from Him nothing came into being that has come into being.
>
> —John 1:1-3

Also, Isaiah 9:6 prophesied that Jesus is "eternal" when prophetically identifying Jesus as "Eternal Father."

It is hard to miss Christ's eternal existence, but many have. It is revealed not only in the New Testament, but even more so in the Old Testament. Unless we thoroughly grasp this profound fact, we trivialize the deity of Christ. If we believe His existence began at Bethlehem, we cannot grasp His magnificence!

The most celebrated event in the Old Testament was clearly the exodus of the Jews from Egypt. Our next lesson will prove that Jesus Christ, as the Angel of the Lord in bodily form, led the Jews away from Pharaoh's clutches. This is stunning, especially to the Jews. In fact, He appeared on more than twelve occasions in the Old Testament as the Angel of the Lord, and at the same was identified as God, as Chapter 12 demonstrates.

Jesus Appeared in Bodily Form on More Than Twelve Occasions in the Old Testament

12

Did Jesus Christ, the Son of God, the Second Godhead of the Trinity, walk and talk on earth in bodily form during the times of the Old Testament? The answer to that question is, yes—clearly, yes. How many of us have to admit that is a truth of which we are not aware?

This study will reveal that Jesus Christ walked and talked on earth in bodily form in Old Testament times when He was identified as the Angel of the Lord, the Angel of His Presence, the Angel of God, and other similar titles. Each time the Angel of the Lord was identified as such, He was also identified as God or Lord and not as a mere angel. The Angel of the Lord appeared in this way on more than twelve separate occasions. The most awesome and compelling appearance was when the Angel of the Lord, in bodily form and identified as God, led and followed the Jews in their exodus from Egypt.

To arrive at the conclusion that the Angel of the Lord is not just a mere angel but is God the Son and is not God the Father or the Holy Spirit, it is necessary to understand what the Hebrew Scriptures as well as the New Testament say about the Trinity of God the Father, God the Son, and God the Holy Spirit. This will help us understand how we can unerringly identify the Angel of the Lord as God the Son. This conclusion can be reached because God the Father and the Holy Spirit are spirits and therefore have no bodily form. The Bible explains that God the Father and God the Holy Spirit are not visible in *bodily* form. We will now learn from the Old Testament that God the Son, described as the Angel of the Lord, was visible in bodily form. This distinction between God the Father and God the Holy Spirit not being visible in bodily form, and only God the Son being visible in bodily form, is essential to understand in this study.

The *Hebrew Scriptures* reveal that the *Trinity* of God the Father, God the Son, and God the Holy Spirit has existed forever, including the times of the Hebrew Scriptures. (God the Son became incarnate—God in an earthly, bodily form—when He was born in Bethlehem.)

To review: we will see that The Angel of the Lord, who was observed in the Hebrew Scriptures on over twelve separate occasions, was identified in the Hebrew Scriptures as God. Because no one can see God the Father and live, the God whom they observed in bodily form as "the Angel of the Lord" was God the Son. And finally, that Jesus Christ, the Angel of the Lord in bodily form, led and followed the exodus of the Jewish people from Egypt.

God the Father Is Spirit and Has No Bodily Form

When speaking to God the Father at Mount Sinai, Moses "saw no form—only a voice" in Deuteronomy 4:11-12:

> "And you came near and stood at the foot of the mountain, and the mountain burned with fire to the very heart of the heavens; darkness, cloud and thick gloom.
>
> "Then the Lord spoke to you from the midst of the fire; you heard the sound of words, but you saw *no form—only a voice*."

Jesus explained that no one has seen the form of God

the Father in John 5:37:

> "And the Father who sent Me, He has borne witness of Me. You have neither heard His voice at any time, *nor seen His form.*"

John also emphasized this in John 1:18:

> *No man has seen God at any time;* the only begotten God, who is in the bosom of the Father, He has explained Him.

Paul likewise explained that "No man has seen or can see" God the Father in 1 Timothy 6:16:

> . . . who alone possesses immortality and dwells in unapproachable light; whom *no man has seen or can see.* To Him be honor and eternal dominion! Amen.

Jesus again taught that God the Father is Spirit in John 4:24:

> "God is spirit, and those who worship Him must worship in spirit and truth."

Jesus, even after His Resurrection, was seen in the same bodily form as when He was identified as the Angel of the Lord. He was not a spirit. "For a spirit does not have flesh and bones as you see that I have," Jesus said in Luke 24:39-40. (See also, John 20:19-20 and 26-27.)

God the Father revealed His glory to Moses and told him that no one would *see Him and live:*

> But He said, "You cannot see My face for no man can see Me and live!"
>
> —Exodus 33:20

The Angel of the Lord Appeared in the Old Testament Over Twelve Times and on Each Occasion Was Identified as God

This study concerning the Angel of the Lord being God becomes profoundly important when we learn that this same Angel of the Lord led and followed the Hebrews in their exodus from Egypt. On over *twelve separate occasions* in the Hebrew Scriptures, the "Angel of the Lord" was seen in bodily form, including His face. On each occasion when "the Angel of the Lord" was identified, such Angel was identified as "God" or "Lord."

To Moses

In Exodus 3:2-6, "the Angel of the Lord" appeared to Moses in a blazing fire "from the midst of a bush." In verses 4, 5, and 6, "the Angel of the Lord" was identified as "God":

> And the Angel of the Lord appeared to Him in a blazing fire from the midst of a bush; and he looked, and behold, the bush was burning with fire, yet the bush was not consumed. So Moses said, "I must turn aside now, and see this marvelous sight, why the bush is not burned up."
>
> When the Lord saw that he turned aside to look, God called to him from the midst of the bush, and said, "Moses, Moses!" And he said, "Here I am." Then He said, "Do not come near here; remove your sandals from your feet, for the place on which you are standing is holy ground."
>
> He said also, "*I am the God* of your father, the God of Abraham, the God of Isaac, and the God of Jacob." Then Moses hid his face, for he was *afraid* to look at God.

Undoubtedly, the "blazing fire" described in the above passage was the glory of God often identified as the Shekinah Glory. The "blazing fire" and the "Angel of the Lord" were described by Luke in Acts 7:30-35 as separate entities.

To Hagar

In Genesis 16:6-13, Hagar, while pregnant with an unnamed child, but later identified as Ishmael, the father of the Arabs, fled from Sarai (Abraham's wife) because, as related in verse 6, "Sarai treated her harshly." This was the beginning of the Arab vs. Jew hostility. "The Angel of the Lord" was talking to Hagar, and in verse 13, and "the Angel of the Lord" was again identified as "God." In view of Exodus 33:20 that no person was allowed to live after seeing God the Father, Hagar was perplexed, as was Moses (Exodus 3:6), and wondered aloud how she could be alive after seeing God when she stated in verse 13, "Have I even remained alive here after seeing Him?" What was not understood by Hagar (and Moses) when she observed the Angel of the Lord, recognizing that He was God, was that she did not see God the Father but, rather, *God the Son*.

> But Abram said to Sarai, "Behold, your maid is in your power; do to her what is good in your sight." So Sarai treated her harshly, and she fled from her presence.
>
> Now the *angel of the Lord* found her by a spring of water in the wilderness, by the spring on the way to Shur. And he said, "Hagar, Sarai's maid, where have you come from and where are you going?" And she said, "I am fleeing from the presence of my mistress Sarai."
>
> Then the angel of the Lord said to her, "Return to your mistress, and submit yourself to her authority."
>
> Moreover, the angel of the Lord said to her, "I will greatly multiply your descendants so that they shall be too many to count." The angel of the Lord said to her further, "Behold, you are with child, and you shall bear a son. And you shall call his name Ishmael, because the Lord has given heed to your affliction.
>
> "And he will be a *wild donkey* of a man, *his hand will*

> *be against everyone*, and everyone's hand will be *against him;* and he will live to the east of all his brothers."
>
> Then she called the name of the Lord who spoke to her, "*Thou art a God who sees*," for she said, "Have I even remained alive here after seeing Him?"
>
> —Genesis 16:6-13

Undoubtedly, Hagar was one of the female servants given by Pharaoh to Abraham to appease Abraham in Genesis 12:16.

Prophecy Concerning the Arabs

As an aside, Genesis 16:12 is a piercingly accurate prophecy concerning the Arabs because Hagar's son, Ishmael, was the first Arab and therefore all Arabs decended from him. This verse foretells what he and his descendants would experience throughout history. This verse prophesied that the Arabs would be a "wild donkey," meaning a nomad; such has proven to be historically accurate, even currently. The same verse also prophesies that "his hand will be against everyone." Again, such prophecy has proven to be accurate, even currently.

Another prophecy in the same verse—"everyone's hand will be against him"—needs no explanation as to its fulfillment, even currently. And finally, "he will live to the east of all his brothers" means living in hostility with them. History has seen a fulfillment of this prophecy even currently, as well as in the Old Testament. See 2 Chronicles 20:23, where Ammon, Moab, and the inhabitants of Mount Sier, all being Arabs, destroyed each other.

To Abraham

In Genesis 22:9-18, "the Angel of the Lord" was talking to Abraham just prior to him preparing to sacrifice his son, Isaac. This same "Angel of the Lord" was identified as God in verses 12, 16, and 17:

> Then they came to the place of which God had told him; and Abraham built the altar there, and

> arranged the wood, and bound his son Isaac, and laid him on the altar on top of the wood.
>
> And Abraham stretched out his hand, and took the knife to slay his son.
>
> But the *angel of the Lord* called to him from heaven, and said, "Abraham, Abraham!" And he said, "Here I am."
>
> And he said, "Do not stretch out your hand against the lad, and do nothing to him; for now I know that you fear God, since you have not withheld your son, your only son, from *Me*."
>
> Then Abraham raised his eyes and looked, and behold, behind him a ram caught in the thicket by his horns; and Abraham went and took the ram, and offered him up for a burnt offering in the place of his son.
>
> And Abraham called the name of that place The Lord Will Provide, as it is said to this day, "In the mount of the Lord it will be provided."
>
> Then the *angel of the Lord* called to Abraham a second time from heaven, and said, "*By Myself* I have sworn, declares the *Lord,* because you have done this thing, and have not withheld your son, your only son. Indeed *I* will greatly bless you, and *I* will greatly multiply your seed as the stars of the heavens, and as the sand which is on the seashore; and your seed shall possess the gate of their enemies. And in your seed all the nations of the earth shall be blessed, because you have obeyed My voice."
>
> —Genesis 22:9-18

Abraham was to sacrifice his son to God, as per God's instructions to him in Genesis 22:1-2. In the same chapter, verse 12, the Angel of the Lord said that Abraham did not withhold this sacrifice "from Me," thus equating the Angel of the Lord with God. The prohibition of God that "no man can see Me and live" was applicable *to seeing God the Father and not to seeing God the Son*. This is clear, because of the number of occasions in the Hebrew Scriptures, God, as the "Angel of the Lord," was seen but the observers lived. In Exodus 33:20, God explained to Moses that "no man can see Me and live." Yet in Exodus 3:2-6, Moses (and as we previously observed Hagar) saw God in the form of the Angel of the Lord and lived.

The Angel of the Lord Led and Followed the Jews in Their Exodus from Egypt

Having now identified "the Angel of the Lord" as Jesus Christ the Son of God, we will now explore the awesome truth that "the Angel of the Lord" in *bodily form* led and followed the Jewish people in their exodus from Egypt. Moses, the author of Exodus, states that it was not just he who led the Jewish people out of Egypt but also the Angel of the Lord:

> And *the Angel of God* who had been going *before* the *camp of Israel*, moved and went behind them and the pillar of cloud moved from before them and stood behind them. So, it came between the camp of Egypt and the camp of Israel; and there was the cloud along with the darkness yet it gave light at night. Thus, the one did not come near the other all night.
>
> —Exodus 14:19-20

And Samuel, the author of Judges, also sets forth that "the Angel of the Lord" brought the Jews out of Egypt by quoting the very words of the Angel of the Lord:

> Now *the Angel of the Lord* came up from Gilgal to Bockim: And He said, "*I brought you up out of Egypt* and *led you* into the land which *I* have sworn to your fathers; and *I* said, '*I* will never break My covenant with you, and as for you, you shall make no covenant with the inhabitants of this land; you

> shall tear down their altars.' But you have not obeyed *Me*, what is this you have done?
>
> "Therefore, *I* also said, '*I* will not drive them out before you; but they shall become as thorns in your sides and their gods shall be a snare to you.' " When *the Angel of the Lord spoke* these words to all the sons of Israel, the people lifted up their voices and wept.
>
> —Judges 2:1-4

The words "My covenant" in verse 2 are telling and revealing. "My covenant" referred to by the Angel of the Lord was the Abrahamic covenant made by God to Abraham in Genesis 12:1-3, and by the Angel of the Lord saying it was "My covenant," the Bible equates yet again the Angel of the Lord with God. Also, in the above passage from Judges, the Angel of the Lord, who we have identified as Christ, the Son of God, affirms that He led the Jewish people out of Egypt.

In talking about the Exodus, God the Father explained that He will send "an angel before you" in Exodus 23:20:

> "Behold, I am going to send *an angel* before you to guard you along the way, and to bring you into the place which I have prepared."

Again, God the Father promised to send "My angel . . . before you" in Exodus 32:34:

> "But go now, lead the people where I told you. Behold, My *angel* shall go before you; nevertheless in the day when I punish, I will punish them for their sin."

And finally, in Isaiah 63:9, Isaiah explained that "the angel of His presence" had "saved them":

> In all their affliction He was afflicted, and *the angel of His presence saved them;* in His love and in *His* mercy He *redeemed them;* and *He* lifted them and carried them all the days of old.

Paul confirms in the New Testament what we now know from the Old Testament: that Christ was the Angel of the Lord who followed the Jewish people in their exodus from Egypt:

> For I do not want you to be unaware, brethren, that our fathers were all under the cloud and all *passed through the sea* and all were baptized into Moses in the cloud and in the sea; and all ate the same spiritual food; and all drank the same spiritual drink, for they were drinking from a *spiritual rock which followed them; and the rock was Christ.*
>
> —1 Corinthians 10:1-4

A more poignant basis for the Jewish people to be comfortable in the presence of Jesus Christ cannot be imagined. All Jewish people who understand this truth that Jesus Christ was responsible for their exodus from Egypt have and will acknowledge Him as their Savior and Messiah.

Other Appearances in the Old Testament of the Angel of the Lord

To Hagar

In Genesis 21:9-18, when Hagar's son Ishmael was approximately eighteen to twenty years old, he was observed by Sarah in verse 9 to be mocking Isaac at his weaning party. Sarah became enraged at this conduct. Isaac, at the time of his weaning, was three to five years of age.

Abraham was 100 years old when Isaac was born (Genesis 21:5), and he was eighty-six years old when Ishmael was born (Genesis 16:16). A Jewish boy was usually weaned when he was three to five years old. Therefore, Ishmael was eighteen to twenty years old when he attended Isaac's weaning feast. Because of this mocking, Sarah instructed Abraham to drive out Hagar and Ishmael. After they left, the Angel of the Lord appeared to Hagar. This was the second time that Hagar encountered the Angel of the Lord, the first time being when Hagar was pregnant with Ishmael as set forth in Genesis 16:6-13.

In Genesis 21:9-18, we read:

> Now Sarah saw the son of Hagar the Egyptian, whom she had borne to Abraham, mocking. Therefore she said to Abraham, "Drive out this maid and her son, for the son of this maid shall not be an heir with my son Isaac." And the matter distressed Abraham greatly because of his son.
>
> But God said to Abraham, "Do not be distressed because of the lad and your maid; whatever Sarah tells you, listen to her, for through Isaac your descendants shall be named. And of the son of the maid I will make a nation also, because he is your descendant."
>
> So Abraham rose early in the morning, and took bread and a skin of water, and gave them to Hagar, putting them on her shoulder, and gave her the boy, and sent her away. And she departed, and wandered about in the wilderness of Beersheba.
>
> And the water in the skin was used up, and she left the boy under one of the bushes. Then she went and sat down opposite him, about a bowshot away, for she said, "Do not let me see the boy die." And she sat opposite him, and lifted up her voice and wept. And God heard the lad crying; and *the angel* of God called to Hagar from heaven, and said to her, "What is the matter with you, Hagar? Do not fear for God has heard the voice of the lad where he is. Arise, lift up the lad, and hold him by the hand; for *I will make a great nation* of him."

The promise in the above verse—that "I will make a great nation of him" by the Angel of the Lord—was not made by a mere angel but God the Son, because only God could make such a promise.

To Jacob

The Angel of the Lord appeared to Jacob in a dream in Genesis 31:11-13:

> "Then *the angel of God* said to me in the dream, 'Jacob,' and I said, 'Here I am.' And he said, 'Lift up, now, your eyes and see that all the male goats which are mating are striped, speckled, and mottled; for I have seen all that Laban has been doing to you. I am the God of Bethel, where you anointed a pillar, where you made a vow to Me; now arise, leave this land, and return to the land of your birth.' "

In the above passage the Angel of the Lord specifically identifies Himself as the "God of Bethel." In Genesis 28:10-15, Jacob had a dream of a ladder "with its top reaching to heaven" and the Lord standing above it. After Jacob awoke, he named this place where he saw this dream as Bethel (Genesis 28:19).

To Gideon

In Judges 6:11-24, the Angel of the Lord appeared to Gideon, and He was identified as "the Lord" in verses 14, 15, 16, 22, and 23, Judges 6:11-24 says:

> Then *the angel of the Lord* came and sat under the oak that was in Ophrah, which belonged to Joash the Abiezrite as his son Gideon was beating out wheat in the wine press in order to save it from the Midianites.
>
> And the *angel of the Lord* appeared to him and said to him, "The Lord is with you, O valiant warrior."

Then Gideon said to him, "O my lord, if the Lord is with us, why then has all this happened to us? And where are all His miracles which our fathers told us about, saying, 'Did not the Lord bring us up from Egypt?' But now the Lord has abandoned us and given us into the hand of Midian."

And the *Lord* looked at him and said, "Go in this your strength and deliver Israel from the hand of Midian. Have *I* not sent you?"

And he said to Him, "O Lord, how shall I deliver Israel? Behold, my family is the least in Manasseh, and I am the youngest in my father's house." But the Lord said to him, "Surely *I* will be with you, and you shall defeat Midian as one man."

So Gideon said to Him, "If now I have found favor in Thy sight, then show me a sign that it is Thou who speakest to me."

"Please do not depart from here, until I come back to Thee, and bring out my offering and lay it before Thee." And He said, "I will remain until you return."

Then Gideon went in and prepared a kid and unleavened bread from an ephah of flour; he put the meat in a basket and the broth in a pot, and brought them out to him under the oak, and presented them.

And the *angel of God* said to him, "Take the meat and the unleavened bread and lay them on this rock, and pour out the broth." And he did so.

Then the *angel of the Lord* put out the end of the staff that was in his hand and touched the meat and the unleavened bread; and *fire sprang* up from the rock and consumed the meat and the unleavened bread. Then the angel of the Lord vanished from his sight.

> When Gideon saw that he was the angel of the Lord, he said, "Alas, O *Lord God!* For now I have *seen the angel of the Lord face to face.*"
>
> And the Lord said to him, "Peace to you, do not fear; you shall not die."
>
> Then Gideon built an altar there to the Lord and named it The Lord is Peace. To this day it is still in Ophrah of the Abiezrites.

To Manoah and His Wife

In Judges 13:2-23, the Angel of the Lord appeared to Manoah, the father of Samson. In verse 11 the Angel of the Lord, when asked who He was, identified Himself as "I am," which in accordance with Exodus 3:14, establishes that the Angel was God.

In verse 18 the Angel of the Lord also said His name was "Wonderful," which is seen in Isaiah 9:6 as another name for Jesus Christ. In verse 22 both Manoah and his wife thought they would surely die because they had seen God. Exodus 33:20 required their death. They, and as we previously learned Moses and Hagar, did not realize that they had not seen God the Father, but rather God the Son:

> And there was a certain man of Zorah, of the family of the Danites, whose name was Manoah; and his wife was barren and had borne no children. Then the *angel of the Lord* appeared to the woman, and said to her, "Behold now, you are barren and have borne no children, but you shall conceive and give birth to a son. Now therefore, be careful not to drink wine or strong drink, nor eat any unclean thing.
>
> "For behold, you shall conceive and give birth to a son, and no razor shall come upon his head, for the boy shall be a Nazirite to God from the womb; and he shall begin to deliver Israel from the hands of the Philistines."
>
> Then the woman came and told her husband,

saying, "A man of God came to me and his appearance was like the appearance of the angel of God, *very awesome*. And I did not ask him where he came from, nor did he tell me his name."

"But he said to me, 'Behold, you shall conceive and give birth to a son, and now you shall not drink wine or strong drink nor eat any unclean thing, for the boy shall be a Nazirite to God from the womb to the day of his death.' "

Then Manoah entreated the Lord and said, "O Lord, please let the man of God whom Thou hast sent come to us again that he may teach us what to do for the boy who is to be born."

And God listened to the voice of Manoah; and the *angel of God* came again to the woman as she was sitting in the field, but Manoah her husband was not with her.

So the woman ran quickly and told her husband, "Behold, the man who came the other day has appeared to me."

Then Manoah arose and followed his wife, and when he came to the man he said to him, "Are you the man who spoke to the woman?" And he said, "*I am*."

And Manoah said, "Now when your words come to pass, what shall be the boy's mode of life and his vocation?"

So the angel of the Lord said to Manoah, "Let the woman pay attention to all that *I* said. She should not eat anything that comes from the vine nor drink wine or strong drink, nor eat any unclean thing; let her observe all that I commanded."

Then Manoah said to the *angel of the Lord*, "Please let us detain you so that we may prepare a kid for you."

And the angel of the Lord said to Manoah, "Though you detain me, I will not eat your food,

> but if you prepare a burnt offering, then offer it to the Lord." For Manoah did not know that he was the angel of the Lord.
>
> And Manoah said to the angel of the Lord, "What is your name, so that when your words come to pass, we may honor you?"
>
> But the angel of the Lord said to him, "Why do you ask my name, seeing it is *wonderful?*"
>
> So Manoah took the kid with the grain offering and offered it to the rock of the Lord, and He performed wonders while Manoah and his wife looked on.
>
> For it came about when the flame went up from the altar toward heaven, that the *angel of the Lord ascended in the flame of the altar.* When Manoah and his wife saw this, they fell on their faces to the ground.
>
> Now the angel of the Lord appeared no more to Manoah or his wife. Then Manoah knew that he was the angel of the Lord.
>
> So Manoah said to his wife, "*We shall surely die, for we have seen God.*"
>
> But his wife said to him, "If the Lord had desired to kill us, He would not have accepted a burnt offering and a grain offering from our hands, nor would He have shown us all these things, nor would He have let us hear things like this at this time."
>
> Then the woman gave birth to a son and named him Samson; and the child grew up and the Lord blessed him. And the Spirit of the Lord began to stir him in Mahaneh-dan, between Zorah and Eshtaol.
>
> —Judges 13:2-27

Sampson was one of three Nazirites identified in the Bible. The strict laws of the Nazirites are set forth in Numbers 6:1-21, which included a prohibition of drinking wine or strong drink or using a razor. The other two Nazirites identified in the Bible are Samuel (1 Samuel 1:1-20) and John the Baptist (Luke 1:5-17). Another interesting fact is that all the mothers of these Nazirites were barren before giving birth to them.

To David

In 1 Chronicles 21:16-18, the Angel of the Lord was seen by David and was identified as God in verse 17:

> Then David lifted up his eyes and saw the *angel of the Lord* standing between earth and heaven, with his drawn sword in his hand stretched out over Jerusalem. Then David and the elders, covered with sackcloth, fell on their faces.
>
> And David said *to* God, "Is it not I who commanded to count the people? Indeed, I am the one who has sinned and done very wickedly, but these sheep, what have they done? O Lord my God, please let Thy hand be against me and my father's household, but not against Thy people that they should be plagued?"
>
> Then the *angel of the Lord commanded Gad to say to David,* that David should go up and build an altar to the Lord on the threshing floor of Ornan the Jebusite.

Psalm 34:7

Psalm 34:7 states:

> The *angel of the Lord* encamps around those who *fear* Him, and *rescues* them.

As God, the Angel of the Lord is to be "feared," and those that fear Him will be rescued.

To Zechariah

In Zechariah 1:12-21, the Angel of the Lord was talking to Zechariah, and in verses 14-17 He identifies Himself as Lord.

In Zechariah 3:1-3, the Angel of the Lord is in heaven and also present is Satan and Joshua. In verse 2, the Angel of the Lord is identified as "the Lord."

In Zechariah 6:4-8, the Angel of the Lord is again talking to Zechariah and identifies Himself as God in verse 8.

A Concluding Thought

We now can see indeed that Jesus Christ, the Messiah—in the person of the Angel of the Lord—was very active in Old Testament times.

Anyone familiar with the Bible, even on a casual basis, knows that Jesus was often referred to as "the Lamb of God." Many, however, do not know that one of these reasons is found in Exodus 12:2-6. Chapter 13 will explain that Jesus presented Himself as the Lamb of God on the the *tenth* day of Nisan—the same date on the calendar that Moses and Aaron in Exodus were instructed to take a lamb for themselves. In addition, Jesus celebrated Passover and was killed on the same date on the calendar that Moses and Aaron were instructed to kill a Passover lamb and celebrate the Passover.

This chapter will result in a deeper understanding of why John the Baptist, when seeing Jesus, said, "Behold the Lamb of God who takes away the sin of the world."

Jesus, the Messiah, Is the Lamb of God, as Prophesied

This chapter is further evidence that Jesus, the Messiah, in the New Testament is the same Messiah and Lamb of God that was prophesied about in the Old Testament.

Isaiah prophesied about the forerunner of Jesus Christ, 750 years before His birth in Isaiah 40:3. This prophecy was fulfilled in Matthew 3:1-6 and John 1:19-23 by John the Baptist. He could not find a more descriptive phrase than to refer to Jesus as the Lamb of God in John 1:29:

> The next day he saw Jesus coming to him, and said, "Behold, the *Lamb of God* who takes away the sin of the world!"

What was the reason that John the Baptist referred to Jesus Christ as the "Lamb of God"? The answer is found through analyzing and understanding the instructions that God gave to Moses and Aaron concerning the "Lamb" and the celebration of Passover in Exodus 12:2-6:

> "This month shall be the beginning of months for you; it is to be the first month of the year to you.
>
> "Speak to all the congregation of Israel, saying, 'On the tenth of this month they are each one to take a *lamb* for themselves, according to their fathers' households, a *lamb* for each household.
>
> 'Now if the household is too small for a lamb, then he and his neighbor nearest to his house are to take one according to the number of persons in them; according to what each man should eat, you are to divide the lamb.
>
> 'Your lamb shall be an *unblemished* male a year old; you may take it from the sheep or from the goats.
>
> 'You shall keep it until the *fourteenth day of the same month*, then the whole assembly of the congregation of Israel is to kill it at twilight.' "
>
> —Exodus 12:2-6

The following chart demonstrates that Jesus, in accordance with the above passage:

1. Presented Himself on Palm Sunday as the Lamb of God on the tenth day of Nisan, the same date that God instructed Moses and Aaron to "take a lamb for themselves."

2. Gave instructions to His disciples to prepare the Passover meal on the *fourteenth* day of Nisan, the same date God instructed Moses and Aaron to prepare the Passover meal.

3. "Reclined" at the Passover table and celebrated Seder—on the *fifteenth* day of Nisan, the same date that God instructed Moses and Aaron to celebrate Seder.

4. Was crucified on the *fifteenth* day of Nisan, the same date that God instructed Moses and Aaron to "kill" the Passover lamb.

Month / Day Jewish Religious Calendar	**Month / Day** Hebrew Scriptures: The Passover Lamb	**Month / Day** New Testament: The Lamb of God
Tenth Day of Nisan[1] Our Sunday	"On the *tenth* day of this month, they are each one to take a lamb for themselves." —Exodus 12:3	Jesus presented Himself as the Lamb of God on Palm Sunday—the *tenth* day of Nisan. —John 12:12-13[2]
Fourteenth Day of Nisan Our Thursday	"And you shall keep it until the *fourteenth* day of the same month. . . ." —Exodus 12:6	Jesus gave instructions to His disciples to prepare to eat the Passover meal—on the fourteenth day of Nisan. —Matthew 26:17-19[3]
Fifteenth Day of Nisan Our Friday	"And then the congregation of Israel is to kill at *twilight.*" —Exodus 12:6[5]	Jesus was crucified on the fifteenth day of Nisan. —Matthew 27:1 and 45[6]
Fifteenth Day of Nisan Our Friday	"And they shall eat the flesh that *same night,* roasted with fire and they shall eat it with unleavened bread and bitter herbs." —Exodus 12:8[5]	Jesus with His disciples "reclined" at the table and ate the Passover meal—on the fifteenth day of Nisan. —Matthew 26:20[4]
Seventeenth Day of Nisan Our Sunday		Jesus was resurrected on the first day of the week—Sunday—the seventeenth day of Nisan. —Matthew 28:1[7]

In sum, Jesus presented Himself as the Lamb of God, on the tenth of Nisan, the same date that God instructed Moses and Aaron to take a lamb for themselves. Jesus celebrated the Passover and was killed on the same date that God instructed Moses and Aaron to kill the lamb and celebrate Passover. If Jesus had not been crucified precisely on Passover, the fifteenth day of Nisan, He would not have been the true Messiah that John the Baptist identified "as the Lamb of God who takes away the sins of the world."

Jesus, being the true Messiah, knew that He must be crucified on Passover when He told His disciples:

> "You know that after two days the *Passover* is coming, and the Son of Man is to be delivered up for *crucifixion*."
>
> —Matthew 26:1-2

Finally, Christ is referred to as "our Passover" in 1 Corinthians 5:7:

> Clean out the old leaven, that you may be a new lump, just as you are in fact unleavened. For *Christ our Passover* also has been sacrificed.

Notes:

[1] The month referred to as "first month of the year" in Exodus 12:2 was the month of Nisan, the first month of the Jewish sacred calendar that corresponds to March and April of our calendar.

[2] Jesus had "supper" at Lazarus' house "six days before the Passover," which would have been the *ninth day* of Nisan (John 12:1). Jesus presented Himself to the multitudes on the "next day" after being at Lazarus' house (Palm Sunday), which would have been the *tenth day* of Nisan:

> On the next day the great multitude who had come to the feast, when they heard that Jesus was coming to Jerusalem, took the branches of the palm trees, and went out to meet Him, and began to cry out, "Hosanna! Blessed is He who comes in the name of the Lord, even the King of Israel."
>
> —John 12:12-13

[3] God instructed Moses and Aaron to celebrate Passover beginning on the fourteenth day of Nisan (Exodus 12:6). Jesus also began to celebrate Passover on the "first day of the Feast," which was the *fourteenth day* of Nisan:

> Now on the *first day* of the Feast of Unleavened Bread the disciples came to Jesus, saying, "Where do You want us to prepare for You to eat the Passover?"
>
> And He said, "Go into the city to a certain man, and say to Him, 'The Teacher says, "My time is at hand; I am to keep the Passover at your house with My disciples." ' "
>
> The disciples did as Jesus had directed them; and they prepared the Passover.
>
> —Matthew 26:17-19

> [4] Now when *evening* had come, He was reclining at table with the twelve disciples.
>
> —Matthew 26:20

Although Passover began on the fourteenth day of Nisan, the actual "reclining at the table" began the "evening" of the fourteenth day of Nisan, which by Jewish reckoning was the *fifteenth day* of Nisan.

[5] By Jewish reckoning a day was from sundown to sundown,

therefore, "twilight" or "night" of the fourteenth day of Nisan would have been the *fifteenth day* of Nisan because it was after sundown.

> [6] Now when *morning* had come, all the chief priests and the elders of the people took counsel against Jesus to put Him to death.
>
> —Matthew 27:1

> Now from the sixth hour darkness fell upon all the land until the ninth hour.
>
> —Matthew 27:45

The "morning" referred to would be the morning after the fourteenth day of Nisan, which was the fifteenth day of Nisan.

> [7] Now after the Sabbath, as it began to dawn toward the first day of the week, Mary Magdalene and the other Mary came to look at the grave.
>
> —Matthew 28:1

Sabbath was on Saturday, and "the first day of the week" would have been Sunday.

Chapter 14 is a study of the end of the age. We are currently experiencing those events constituting the end of the age. As we will learn, Christ returns after the last of these prophetic events has occured.

The End of the Age: A Study of Prophetic Events Leading to the Second Advent of Christ

Several years ago, in conjunction with a biblical tour of Israel, I was staying in a kibbutz on the shores of the Sea of Galilee. Everyone had gone to bed. I decided to go to a tavern in the kibbutz. While at this tavern, I began a discussion with the bartender concerning the evidence for the deity of Christ. As the discussion heated up, we drew a crowd. I discussed in particular with the bartender, many of the Messianic prophecies previously set forth in this paper.

After these prophecies were presented, the bartender said, "That's all well and good, but I would be persuaded if the prophecies that were made thousands of years ago were being fulfilled within the last seventy-five years and particularly within my lifetime." That is precisely what is revealed in the study of eschatology, also known as the study of the end of the age. I then discussed many of the prophecies that we will now study in this chapter—prophecies that sent the bartender and others in the tavern reeling. They eventually understood that all of these prophecies concerning the end of the age were made 2,000 to 3,500 years ago, with the first three being fulfilled within the last twenty-two to seventy-five years. They also understood that if the Bible accurately predicted 2,000 to 3,500 years ago events that had already occurred preceding the end of the age, then it was equally clear that those prophecies that are yet to occur *would* occur. They also understood that only God could so prophesy.

The study of the events that will precede the end of the age also involves the study of the second coming of Jesus Christ. This is true because the end of the age will be followed by the second coming of Jesus Christ, which will in turn usher in the Messianic Kingdom. Nowhere does the Bible teach the end of the world but rather, only the end of the age. The Bible teaches that Earth will not end, but rather will exist in a totally different form.

Some Christian authors have utilized what can be called "newspaper exegesis," which is seeing something occurring in current events and cramming it into God's Word. Rather prophecy should be studied and thereafter applied to current events as they happen. Such prophecy must fit perfectly and comfortably into the biblical passage without using "newspaper exegesis". God's Word does teach us that we are presently in the latter days leading to the end of the age. The following are those events that have taken place or will take place ushering in the end of the age. The first three events have been fulfilled as prophesied.

First Event: World Wars

Our Lord prophesied that the first event to usher in the end of the age would be *world wars*.

> And Jesus came out from the temple and was going away when His disciples came up to point out the temple buildings to Him.
>
> And He answered and said to them, "Do you not see all these things? Truly I say to you, not one stone here shall be left upon another, which will not be torn down."
>
> And as He was sitting on the Mount of Olives, the disciples came to Him privately, saying, "Tell us, when will these things be, and what will be the sign

> of Your coming, *and of the end of the age?*"
>
> And Jesus answered and said to them, "See to it that no one misleads you. For many will come in My name, saying, I am the Christ, and will mislead many. And you will be hearing of wars and rumors of wars; see that you are not frightened, for those things must take place, but that is not yet the end. For *nation will rise against nation, and kingdom against kingdom*, and in various places there will be *famines and earthquakes*. But all these things are merely the beginning of *birth pangs*."
>
> —Matthew 24:1-8

In verses one and two above, Jesus prophesied that the temple would be destroyed, which occurred in 70 A.D. (See page 27.)

In verse three, Jesus was asked three questions:

1. When will the *temple* be destroyed?
2. What would be the sign of Jesus' *second coming?*
3. What would be the signs of the *end of the age?*

Jesus responds to the latter question in verses four through eight. In verses four through six, Jesus sets forth what will not be signs of the end of the age, rather business as usual, the presence of false Messiahs, and local wars.

In verse seven, Jesus does respond as to what will mark the beginning of the end of the age as follows:

1. Nation will rise against nation and kingdom against kingdom.
2. Famines.
3. Earthquakes.

In verse eight, Jesus refers to these events as "merely the beginning of birth *pangs*." He explained about birth pangs in John 16:20-22, that "whenever a woman is in travail she has sorrow because her hour has come, but when she gives birth to the child she remembers the anguish no more, for joy that a child has been born into the world."

Similarly, "birth pangs" bringing forth the "end of the age" will have "travail," but the end of the age ushering in the second advent of Christ and the Messianic Kingdom and thereafter eternity will bring joy. To repeat, the end of the age will therefore go through a series of birth pangs having "travail" before giving birth to the second advent of Christ, followed by the Messianic Kingdom and then eternity, which will both bring joy.

It is necessary to distinguish in verse seven that "nation will rise against nation and kingdom against kingdom" from "wars and rumors of wars" in verse six. Throughout history there has been "wars and rumors of wars."

The phrase, "nation will rise against nation" and "kingdom against kingdom" is a Jewish idiom for a worldwide conflict. Dr. Arnold Fruchtenbaum said in *The Footsteps of the Messiah* on page 64:

> In Christ's day the expression of nation against nation, kingdom against kingdom was a Jewish idiom of a world war preceding the coming of the Messiah. *The Bereshit Rabbah XL* 11:4 states: "If you shall see kingdoms rising against each other in turn then give heed and note the *footsteps of the Messiah*."

Other passages in the Hebrew Scriptures indicate when the phrases "nation will rise against nation" and "kingdom against kingdom" are used, this points to a total conflict of the area in view. See Isaiah 19:1-4 and 2 Chronicles 15:1-7.

Chapter 24 of Matthew also points throughout to a worldwide view, and verse seven also indicates that worldwide view by referring to a global conflict. See Matthew 24:14, 21, 30, and 31. We now know that the first worldwide conflict was the First World War, the "War to End All Wars" that began in 1914, and therefore was the event that Jesus prophesied would usher in the end of the age. Also in verse 7, Jesus prophesied that the end of the age would be ushered in by "famines and earthquakes."

The *Encyclopedia Americana* indicates that from 63 A.D. to 1896, there were just twenty-six recorded earthquakes. Thereafter, the increased incidents of earthquakes are common knowledge. From 1970 to date, it does not take much reflection to remember a series of devastating earthquakes throughout California, particularly in San Francisco, Palm Springs, and Yucca Valley, as well as Turkey, Japan, China, and rest of the world.

In reference to famines, we see on television daily the increased starvation in Ethiopia, India, Sudan, Bangladesh, and throughout the Third World.

Second Event: Worldwide Gathering of the Jews

The next chronological event or birth pang after the world war would be the *first* worldwide gathering of the Jewish people to Israel. This worldwide gathering was prophesied in the following passages from Ezekiel, written hundreds of years before the birth of Jesus:

> "As I live," declares the Lord God, "surely with a mighty hand and with an outstretched arm and *with wrath poured out*, I shall be king over you. And I shall bring *you out* from the peoples and gather you from the lands where you are *scattered*, with a mighty hand and with an outstretched arm and with wrath poured out; and I shall bring you into the wilderness of the peoples, and there I shall enter into judgment with you face to face. As I entered into judgment with your fathers in the wilderness of the land of Egypt, so I will enter into judgment with you," declares the Lord God.
>
> —Ezekiel 20:33-36

> And the word of the Lord came to me saying, "Son of man, the house of Israel has become dross to Me; all of them are bronze and tin and iron and lead in the furnace; they are the dross of silver.
>
> "Therefore, thus says the Lord God, 'Because all of you have become dross, therefore, *behold, I am*

> *going to gather you into the midst of Jerusalem.* As they gather silver and bronze and iron and lead and tin into the furnace to blow fire on it in order to melt it, so *I shall gather you in* My *anger and in* My *wrath*, and I shall lay you there and melt you.
>
> 'I will gather you and blow on you with the fire of My wrath, and you will be melted in the midst of it. As silver is melted in the furnace, so you will be melted in the midst of it; and you will know that I, the Lord, have poured out My *wrath* on you.' "
>
> —Ezekiel 22:17-22

The above two passages in Ezekiel refer to the gathering of His chosen people in preparation for the judgment of the Tribulation (Revelation 6-19) and not a blessing.

We have witnessed the fulfillment of this prophecy by the first worldwide gathering of the Jews, which culminated in the re-establishment of the state of Israel on May 14, 1948, when Israel was declared to be an independent sovereign state.

The following passages set forth the regathering of the Jews at the end of the age. This second gathering will not be for judgment but for the blessing of entering the Messianic Kingdom.

> Then the Lord your God will restore you from captivity, and have compassion on you, and will gather you *again* from all the peoples where the Lord your God has scattered you.
>
> If your outcasts are at the ends of the earth, from there the Lord your God will gather you, and from there He will bring you back.
>
> And the Lord your God will bring you into the land which your fathers possessed, and you shall possess it; and He will prosper you and multiply you more than your fathers.
>
> —Deuteronomy 30:3-5

> Then it will happen on that day that the Lord will *again* recover the *second time* with His hand the remnant of His people, who will remain from Assyria, Egypt, Pathros, Cush, Elam, Shinar, Hamath, and from the islands of the sea.
>
> And He will lift up a standard for the nations, and will assemble the banished ones of Israel, and will gather the dispersed of Judah from the four corners of the earth.
>
> —Isaiah 11:11-12

Third Event: Jerusalem Under Jewish Control

After the first worldwide gathering of the Jewish people and the re-establishment of the state of Israel, the next chronological event before the end of the age would be the capture of the old city of Jerusalem from Jordan. Four passages require the *rebuilding* of the third Jewish temple, which in turn requires the old city of Jerusalem to be under *Jewish control.* This temple can only be built in the old city of Jerusalem. These passages speak of this temple being in existence. Each of these prophecies requires the temple being in existence no later than the middle of the Tribulation, which lasts for seven years (as described in Revelation chapters 6-19).

> And he will make a firm covenant with the many for one week, but in the *middle* of the week he will put a *stop to sacrifice* and grain offering; and on the wing of abominations will come one who makes desolate, even until a complete destruction, one that is decreed, is poured out on the one who makes desolate.
>
> —Daniel 9:27

The fulfillment of this passage could not occur until the temple is built because this "sacrifice" can only be made in the temple, and the rebuilding cannot occur until the old city of Jerusalem is under the *control* of Israel. This building of the temple must be completed three-and-a-half years before the end of the Tribulation. "Week" refers to the seven-year tribulation that immediately precedes the return of Christ. "In the middle of the week" refers to the three-and-a-half year period before the return of Christ.

The second prophecy, this time by Jesus, requiring the temple to be built says:

> "Therefore when you see the abomination of desolation which was spoken of through Daniel the prophet, *standing in the holy place*. . . ."
>
> —Matthew 24:15

Matthew 24:15 is a reference by Jesus to the "abomination of desolation" spoken of by Daniel the prophet (Daniel 9:27) that will be standing in the "holy place" by the middle of the Tribulation. The "holy place" can only be located in the temple, which, of course, requires it to be built. For the temple to be rebuilt, Jerusalem must be under the control of Israel.

The third prophecy requiring the temple to be built goes like this:

> Let no one in any way deceive you, for it will not come unless the *apostasy* comes first, and the man of lawlessness is revealed, the son of destruction, who opposes and exalts himself above every so-called god or object of worship, so that he takes his seat in the temple of God, displaying himself as being God.
>
> —2 Thessalonians 2:3-4

The above passage talks about the antichrist, before the second advent, taking his seat in "*the temple of God*"—a temple cannot exist until it is built, and it cannot be built until Jerusalem is under the control of Israel.

The fourth prophecy requiring the temple to be built reads:

> And there was given me a measuring rod like a staff; and someone said, "Rise and measure the *temple of* God, and the altar, and those who worship in it. And leave out the court which is outside *the temple*, and do not measure it, for it has been given to the nations; and they will tread under foot the holy city for forty-two months."
>
> —Revelation 11:1-2

This passage again refers "to the temple of God" being in existence by the middle of the Tribulation, which yet again requires Jerusalem to be *controlled* by Israel.

The fulfillment of these prophecies requiring the old city of Jerusalem being under the control of Israel occurred when Israel, during the Six Day War of 1967, *captured* the old city of Jerusalem and other contiguous territory, which had been under Jordanian control.

The stage is now set for the building of the temple as required in the above passages, which could occur at any time. Thus, the third birth pang preceding the end of the age has transpired.

The above three birth pangs preceding the end of the age *have occurred*, and the following birth pangs *will* occur.

Fourth Event: The Invasion of Israel

The next event to usher in the end of the age, according to Ezekiel 38:1-39:16, is the Russian invasion of Israel. In this invasion, Russia (not including the former Soviet federated states) will be joined by Iran, Ethiopia, Somalia, Germany, and Armenia.

The fact that this event occurs after the second birth pang, which is the worldwide gathering of the Jews, is brought out in Ezekiel 38:8:

> In the latter days you will come into the land . . . whose inhabitants have been gathered from many nations. . . .

Therefore, this invasion can only occur "in the latter days" after this gathering.

The Nations Who Will Be Involved in This Invasion

Ezekiel 38:1-6 describes who will be involved in this invasion:

> And the word of the Lord came to me saying, "Son of man, set your face toward Gog of the land of *Magog*, the prince of *Rosh*, *Meshech*, and *Tubal*, and prophesy against him, and say, 'Thus says the Lord God, "Behold, I am against you, O Gog, prince of Rosh, Meshech, and Tubal. And I will turn you about, and put hooks into your jaws, and I will bring you out, and all your army, horses and horsemen, all of them splendidly attired, a great company with buckler and shield, and all of them wielding swords; *Persia*, *Ethiopia*, and *Put* [Somalia] with them, all of them with shield and helmet; Gomer [Germany] with all its troops; *Beth-togarmah* [Armenia] from the remote parts of the north with all its troops—many peoples with you." ' "

Gog, in the above passage, describes an unidentified leader of Russia whose identity will not be known until this invasion occurs. Magog, Meshech, and Tubal were tribes living between the Black and Caspian Seas in what is now Southern Russia. The tribe of Rosh lived in what is now Northern Russia. Collectively these tribes occupied what is now known as Russia. This description does not encompass all of the formerly existing Federated States of the Soviet Union. It does encompass what is now known as Soviet Russia after the Federation was dismantled.

Thus, the eschatological time clock is set.

The following countries will join Russia in this invasion: Persia (Iran), Ethiopia, Put (Somalia), Gomer (Germany), and Beth Togarmah (Armenia).

Where This Invasion Occurs

Ezekiel 38:7-9 identifies where this invasion is to occur:

> "Be prepared, and prepare yourself, you and all your companies that are assembled about you, and be a guard for them. After many days you will be summoned; in the latter years you will come into the land that is restored from the sword, whose inhabitants have been gathered from many nations to the *mountains of Israel* which had been a continual waste; but its people were brought out from the nations, and they are living securely, all of them. And you will go up, you will come like a storm; you will be like a cloud covering the land, you and all your troops, and many peoples with you."

The "mountains of Israel" surround Jerusalem and extend from approximately the southern tip of the Sea of Galilee to the southern tip of the Dead Sea. Such mountains cannot be in Israel until Israel has been declared a state. Thus, this prophecy cannot be fulfilled until all three birth pangs previously discussed have been fulfilled—world war, the formation of the state of Israel, and the control of the city of Jerusalem by Israel. This control after the 1967 war, as previously discussed, included not only the old city of Jerusalem, but also the entire West Bank formerly controlled by Jordan, including the "mountains of Israel."

Why This Invasion Occurs

The *reason* for this invasion is described in Ezekiel 38:10-13:

> Thus says the Lord God, "It will come about on that day, that thoughts will come into your mind, and you will devise an evil plan, and you will say, 'I will go up against the land of *unwalled villages*. I will go against those who are at rest, that live securely, all of them living without walls, and having no bars or gates, *to capture spoil* and *to seize plunder*, to turn your hand against the waste places which are now inhabited, and against the people who are gathered from the nations, who have acquired cattle and goods, who live at the center of the world.'
>
> "Sheba and Dedan and the merchants of Tarshish with all its villages will say to you, 'Have you come to capture spoil?' Have you assembled your company to seize plunder, to carry away silver and gold, to take away cattle and goods, to capture great spoil?' "

In the above passage God is talking to Gog, the unidentified leader of Russia. The answer as to why this invasion occurs is set forth in verse 12: "to capture spoil." It is known that the Dead Sea contains billions of tons of sodium, chlorine, sulfur, potassium, magnesium, and bromide. Israel is also a pathway to massive oil reserves.

How the Invaders Are Destroyed

Ezekiel 38:17-23 describes the invading hoards being destroyed and the manner of their destruction:

> Thus says the Lord God, "Are you the one of whom I spoke in former days through My servants the prophets of Israel, who prophesied in those days for many years that I would bring you against them? And it will come about on that day, when Gog

> comes against the land of Israel," declares the Lord God, "that My fury will mount up in My anger. And in My zeal and in My blazing wrath I declare that on that day there will surely be a *great earthquake* in the land of Israel.
>
> "And the fish of the sea, the birds of the heavens, the beasts of the field, all the creeping things that creep on the earth, and all the men who are on the face of the earth will shake at My presence; the mountains also will be thrown down, the steep pathways will collapse, and every wall will fall to the ground.
>
> "I will call for a sword against him on all My mountains," declares the Lord God. "Every man's sword will be against his brother. *With pestilence* and with blood I shall enter into judgment with him; and I shall rain on him and on his troops, and on the many peoples who are with him, a torrential rain, with hailstones, fire, and brimstone.
>
> "And I shall magnify Myself, sanctify Myself, and make Myself known in the sight of many nations; and they will know that I am the Lord."

The invading army will be destroyed by pestilence, torrential rain, hailstorms, fire, brimstone, and civil war (verse 22). The reason for such means of destruction is to glorify God and not man, which would surely occur if the army of Israel was responsible for their destruction (verse 23).

In sum, evidence that the stage is set for this invasion is clear from the fact that Ethiopia was pro-Israel until Haile Selassie was deposed and Iran under the Shah was pro-Israel until the Islamic Revolution occurred and Khomeini took power. It could not be imagined that Germany would join Russia in doing anything prior to the division of East and West Germany, but those two countries were reunified with the fall of the Berlin Wall in 1989. Armenia is not now, as formerly, located in Turkey (a country that is closely aligned presently with the United States), which would allow for Armenia's participation. The invasion by Russia, rather than the entire Soviet Union, is now possible because of the dismantling of the Soviet Union and the establishment of Russia as an independent state.

Some other interesting observations concerning this invasion:

• Ezekiel 38:11 describes Israel as living in "unwalled villages," which is a description of a kibbutz.

• Ezekiel 39:6 describes *Russia itself* being devastated by brimstone.

• Ezekiel 39:7-8 describes Israel as being sanctified among the Gentile nations.

The nations involved in this invasion will be Russia, Iran, Ethiopia, Somalia, Germany, and Armenia. The absence of any Arab states is remarkable. Unfolding before our eyes is evidence that the Arab states will not be a part of this invasion because peace has been made between Israel, Egypt, and Jordan. Also, Iraq was recently conquered during Operation Iraqi Freedom, precluding their involvement. At the time of this writing, negotiations are underway for a peace treaty between Israel and Palestine.

Also, the Arabs were undoubtedly discouraged by their singular lack of success in the War for Independence in 1948-49; the Six Day War in 1967, and the war in 1973.

Fifth Event: One World Government

The next event after the invasion of Israel before the end of the age will be the formation of a one-world government from the fourth Gentile nation. In order to understand this prophetic event, it will be necessary to understand, in at least a superficial fashion, the vision of Daniel:

> In the first year of Belshazzar king of Babylon Daniel saw a dream and visions in his mind as he lay on his bed; then he wrote the dream down and

related the following summary of it.

Daniel said, "I was looking in my vision by night, and behold, the four winds of heaven were stirring up the great sea. And *four great beasts* were coming up from the sea, different from one another. The first was like a lion and had the wings of an eagle. I kept looking until its wings were plucked, and it was lifted up from the ground and made to stand on two feet like a man; a human mind also was given to it.

"And behold, *another beast*, a *second one*, resembling a *bear*. And it was raised up on one side, and three ribs were in its mouth between its teeth; and thus they said to it, 'Arise, devour much meat!' After this I kept looking, and behold, *another one*, like a *leopard*, which had on its back four wings of a bird; the beast also had four heads, and dominion was given to it.

"After this I kept looking in the night visions, and behold, *a fourth beast*, *dreadful and terrifying* and extremely strong; and it had large iron teeth. It devoured and crushed, and trampled down the remainder with its feet; and it was different from all the beasts that were before it, and it had ten horns.

"While I was contemplating the horns, behold, another horn, a little one, came up among them, and three of the first horns were pulled out by the roots before it; and behold, this horn possessed eyes like the eyes of a man and a mouth uttering great boasts."

—Daniel 7:1-8

Although it appears difficult to understand, the following is the interpretation of this vision: Verse 2 describes "the sea," which is the Mediterranean and probably symbolizes the Gentile world.

The *first beast* described in verse 4 is the Babylonian Empire. Described in verse 5 is a *bear,* which is the Medo-Persian Empire. Verse 6 describes a leopard, which is the Grecian Empire and is consistent with the Alexander the Great conquests being performed with leopard-like speed from 336 B.C. to 323 B.C. Verse 7 describes the Roman Empire, which would include the fourth Gentile nation. Thus, this is a prophetic worldview of history by Daniel, who lived during the Babylonian Empire. He prophesied that following the Babylonian Empire, we would see sequentially the Medo-Persian Empire, the Grecian Empire, and the Roman Empire, or fourth Gentile nation. We are currently still in the times of the fourth Gentile nation. It is from this nation that the one-world government will arise.

Daniel 7:23 describes the formation of a *one-world government* prior to the end of the age:

> "Thus He said: 'The fourth beast will be a fourth kingdom on the earth, which will be different from all the other kingdoms, and it will devour the *whole earth* and tread it down and crush it.' "

Thus, the fourth kingdom will devour the whole earth, giving rise to a one-world government.

Sixth Event: Ten Kingdoms

From this one-world government will arise ten kingdoms, as set forth in Daniel 7:24. One author through the use of "newspaper exegesis" has interpreted the fulfillment of this prophecy by the formation of the Common Market in Europe, which at the time of his interpretation had ten member nations. This is an example of newspaper exegesis being the attempt to cram into prophecies current events, rather than allowing current events to fit comfortably into such prophecies. Such newspaper exegesis resulted in the false interpretations that the Common Market (or EU, the European Union) fulfilled the prophecy of the ten kingdoms, which, as of this writing, numbers *fifteen* nations. In addition, the EU has invited eight countries from Central and Eastern Europe, plus Cyprus and Malta, to join the organization in 2004.

The following passage, however, indicates that the ten kingdoms will come from the *whole world* and *not just Europe*. Moreover, events four and five must precede the arise of the ten kingdoms.

> "As for the ten horns, [the antichrist] out of this kingdom [one-world government] ten kings will arise; and another will arise after them, and he will be different from the previous ones and will subdue three kings."
>
> —Daniel 7:24

Other Events

Time and your patience do not allow for a discussion of the final chronological birth pangs following the ten kingdoms, which are: (7) the appearance of the antichrist (Daniel 7:24 and 27 and 2 Thessalonians 2:1-3); (8) a period of false peace and security (1 Thessalonians 5:1-3); (9) a covenant between the antichrist and Israel (Daniel 9:27); (10) the tribulation (Revelation 6-19); and (11) the second advent of Christ (Matthew 24:29-31).

The second advent of Christ is one of the most momentous events of His life as will be seen in the next heading.

Where Christ Returns Upon His Second Advent

The first activity of Jesus Christ upon His second advent at the end of the age will be to return initially and annihilate the forces of the antichrist at Bozrah, which is located in present-day Petra in southern Jordan, where He will single-handedly eliminate them:

> Who is this who comes from Edom, with garments of glowing colors from Bozrah, this One who

> is majestic in His apparel, marching in the greatness of His strength?
>
> "It is I who speak in righteousness, mighty to save."
>
> Why is your apparel red, and Your garments like the one who treads in the wine press?
>
> "I have trodden the wine trough alone, and from the peoples there was no man with Me. I also trod them in My anger. And trampled them in My wrath; and their lifeblood is sprinkled on My garments, and I stained all My raiment.
>
> "For the day of vengeance was in My heart, and My year of redemption has come.
>
> "I looked, and there was no one to help, and I was astonished and there was no one to uphold; so My own arm brought salvation to Me; and My wrath upheld Me.
>
> "I trod down the peoples in My anger, and made them drunk in My wrath, and I poured out their lifeblood on the earth."
>
> —Isaiah 63:1-6

The person speaking in the above passage is Jesus Christ. He explains that He alone will annihilate the forces of the antichrist, and because of this annihilation His garments will be "red" from their blood.

The antichrist previously will have attacked the Jews located in Bozrah because in the middle of the tribulation Jesus instructed them to "flee to the mountains" (Bozrah):

> "Therefore when you see the *abomination of desolation* which was spoken of through Daniel the prophet, standing in the holy place (let the reader understand), then let those who are in Judea flee to the mountains [Bozrah]."
>
> —Matthew 24:15-16

Non-Chronological Events that Must Also Occur Before the Tribulation

The following events must also occur before the tribulation, the chronology of which cannot be determined:

1. Blackouts. (Joel 2:31)
2. The return of Elijah. (Malachi 4:5-6)
3. The Rapture. (1 Thessalonians 4:13-18)
4. The building of third temple in Jerusalem. (Matthew 24:15 and 2 Thessalonians 4:13-18)
5. Jesus also explained that before the end of the age, the gospel must be preached to the whole world, establishing His desire that the whole world would have knowledge of the truth and therefore have the opportunity to be saved from the lake of fire (Matthew 24:14).

In studying these prophecies concerning the end times, I was profoundly influenced by the fact that they were written 2,000 to 3,500 years ago and because there has been a fulfillment of the prophecies concerning World War I, the regathering of the Israeli people, and the capturing of Jerusalem. It became clear to me, as it did to the bartender, because the first three birth pangs have occurred exactly as prophesied, that the subsequent events as prophesied will likewise occur. Pertinent to this conclusion is that the historical stage is set for the next event, which is the invasion of Israel.

In the next chapter, we will see that the truth of the Crucifixion and Resurrection was unwittingly proved by secular historians.

The Crucifixion and Resurrection of Jesus: Fact or Fiction? 15

Tom Anderson, former president of the California Trial Lawyers Association and co-author of *The Basic Advocacy Manual of the Association of Trial Lawyers of America*, says, "Let's assume that Christ did not rise from the dead. Let's assume that the written accounts of His appearances to hundreds of people are false. I want to pose a question. With an event so well-publicized, don't you think that it's reasonable that one historian, one eyewitness, one antagonist would record for all time that he had seen Christ's body? 'Listen, I saw that tomb—it was not empty! Look, I was there, Christ did not rise from the dead. As a matter of fact, I saw Christ's body.' The silence of history is deafening when it comes to testimony against the Resurrection."

—from *The Resurrection Factor* by Josh McDowell (Here's Life Publishers, Inc., 1981, pg. 66)

I enjoyed being quoted in a book by Josh McDowell, but what's more important to me is establishing that the crucifixion and resurrection of Jesus Christ has a historical face; otherwise, our faith is in vain, which Paul admitted in 1 Corinthians 15:12-19. Either the crucifixion and resurrection of Jesus Christ was a heartless and contrived hoax, or it was the most convincing, compelling, and meaningful truth in history. Everyone when considering the truth of the Crucifixion and Resurrection is literally on *trial for their lives*, as explained by Paul:

> That if you confess with your mouth Jesus as Lord, and believe in your heart that *God raised Him from the dead*, you shall be saved.
>
> —Romans 10:9

Thus Paul explains that we won't be saved unless we believe that "God raised Him [Jesus] from the dead." God provides, as discussed in this chapter, overwhelming evidence of Jesus' ressurection from the dead. If I, as a trial lawyer, was retained to prove that either the trial, death, and resurrection of Jesus was a hoax or was the truth, my first task would be to attempt to find witnesses to this Crucifixion and Resurrection and interview them. Also I would attempt to identify historical documents concerning these events. This investigation would be conducted in the same way as any other investigation in my office. I would instruct my investigators to interview eyewitnesses and identify such documents to this alleged Crucifixion and Resurrection.

Have such investigations occurred? Were such interviews conducted? The answer is—yes! Who conducted such investigations and such interviews? Historians, that's who. They are in the business of interviewing witnesses, examining documents, and recording their findings, which they did.

Sources of Witnesses to the Truth

The trial, crucifixion, burial, and resurrection of Jesus

occurred in a space-time dimension before *thousands* of witnesses in Jerusalem. It was not a hallucination. It was anticipated by the Jews for centuries through the following prophecies, and such witnesses would be available for historians to interview and record their findings:

> A band of evil doers has encompassed me; they *pierced my hands and my feet*. I can count all my bones. They look, they stare at me; they *divide my garments among them* and for my clothing they cast lots.

Anyone in the literate world, upon reading the above passage, can identify this event as the crucifixion of Jesus, and rightly so. It is supernatural that this prophecy was written by King David over a thousand years before the Crucifixion in Psalm 22:16-18. Jews in Jerusalem, at the time of Jesus' crucifixion, were likewise aware of this prophecy, and for these same thousand years had anticipated its fulfillment by the Messiah. When Jesus claimed to be this Messiah, *everyone in Jerusalem would be potential witnesses* to this anticipated crucifixion.

> Surely, our griefs He Himself bore, and our sorrows He carried; yet, we, ourselves esteemed Him stricken, smitten of God and afflicted. But He was *pierced through for our transgressions, He was crushed for our iniquities*; the chastening for our well-being fell upon Him, and by His scourging we are healed. All of us like sheep have gone astray, each of us has turned to his own way; but the Lord has caused the *iniquity of us all to fall on Him*.
>
> —Isaiah 53:4-6

The New Testament states that Jesus did die, and the Hebrew Scriptures prophesied that Jesus would die on the cross for the sins of all believers and unbelievers (1 John 2:2). The above prophecy 700 years before Jesus' birth foretold that the Messiah would be "pierced and crushed" for our sins and that we would be healed by His "scourging" (whipping). All of this—whipping and piercing—occurred before *thousands of witnesses* who were available for historians to interview.

> And I will pour out on the house of David and on the inhabitants of Jerusalem, the spirit of grace and of supplication, so that they will look upon me whom *they have pierced;* and they will mourn for Him, as one mourns for an only son, and they will weep bitterly over Him like the bitter weeping over a first born.
>
> —Zechariah 12:10

The above prophecy by the Jewish prophet Zechariah was written 500 years before the crucifixion of Jesus. It foretold that the inhabitants of Jerusalem, after Jesus' crucifixion, would mourn and weep bitterly over Him. All of these were *available as witnesses* for historians to interview.

There were six separate trials of Jesus. *The three Jewish trials* were religious ones where Jesus was falsely accused of the crime of blasphemy. These trials were before Annas (John 18:13), Caiaphus (John 18:24), and the Sanhedrin (Luke 22:66). Thereafter, there were *three Roman trials*, which were political ones where Jesus was falsely accused, but this time He was convicted of the crime of instigating a rebellion against Caesar. They were before Pilate (Luke 23:1), Herod (Luke 23:7-10), and again Pilate (Luke 23: 11-12). All of these trials were public, and *all such witnesses* to these trials were available for historians to interview.

> His grave was assigned with wicked men. Yet, He was with a *rich man* in His death.
>
> —Isaiah 53:9

The above prophecy by Isaiah 700 years before the Crucifixion was fulfilled in Matthew 27:57-60 when Joseph of

Arimathea, a "rich man" and member of the Sanhedrin, asked Pontius Pilate for the body of Jesus so he could lay it in "his own new tomb" (Matthew 27:60). Thus, He was "with a rich man in His death" (Isaiah 53:9). Before this intervention by Joseph of Arimathea, Jesus, together with the two criminals who were also crucified with Him, was destined to be buried "with wicked men" in a graveyard reserved for criminals outside Jerusalem. Thus, not only was the trial and crucifixion of Jesus prophesied but also *His burial place*. Again, *thousands of witnesses* in Jerusalem knew and anticipated this tomb and would have been interviewed by historians to determine first, if Jesus was buried in such tomb and second, if such tomb was empty after His Resurrection.

Secular Historians Have Recorded that the Crucifixion and Resurrection of Christ Are Well-Established Historical Facts

> Non-Christian sources are meager and contribute nothing to the history of Jesus that is not already known from the Christian tradition. The mention of Jesus' *execution* in the *Annals of Roman historian, Tacitus* (XV, 44) written about A.D. 110, is nevertheless worthy of note. In his account of the persecution of Christians under the Emperor Nero, which was occasioned by the burning of Rome (A.D. 64), the Emperor, to rid himself of suspicion, blamed the fire on the so-called Christians who were already hated among the people. Tacitus writes in explanation: "The name is derived from *Christ* whom the procurator, Pontius Pilate, had executed in the reign of Tiberius . . ." The passage only affords *proof of the ignominious end and (crucifixion) of Jesus* as the founder of a religious movement and illustrates the common opinion of that movement in Rome.
>
> —*Encyclopedia Britannica,* volume 10, page 145

Historians (investigators) such as Tacitus have examined

documents, talked to witnesses, and recorded their findings. The *Encyclopedia Britannica* records as a *historical fact* that Jesus was crucified by Pontius Pilate. The author of this article on Jesus Christ was Dr. Gunther Bornkamm, professor of New Testament Studies, Rupert Charles University of Heidelberg and author of *Jesus of Nazareth:*

> *In the Talmud*, a compendium of Jewish law, lore and commentary, only a few statements of the rabbis [Jewish religious leaders] of the first and second centuries come into consideration. Containing mostly polemics or Jewish Apologetics, they reveal an acquaintance with the Christian tradition but include several divergent legendary motifs as well. The picture of Jesus offered in these writings may be summarized as follows: . . . *and was hanged (crucified) on the eve of the Passover.*
>
> —*Encyclopedia Britannica*, volume 10, page 145

Thus, the Jewish Talmud, written after the Crucifixion by Jewish scribes who were antagonists of Jesus, admitted that Jesus was "hanged (crucified) on the eve of the Passover."

> Pontius Pilate, who is designated in an inscription found in 1961 as praefectus Judaeae, ruled (A.D. 26-36) ruthlessly and with bursts of cruelty.
>
> —*Encyclopedia Britannica*, volume 10, page 147

Until 1961 the only references to Pontius Pilate were literary. Because he played such a central role in the Crucifixion, the question would arise: Did he actually exist, or was he a fabrication? The above quote from the *Encyclopedia Britannica* establishes that Pontius Pilate was a historical figure.

> The most important point in its favor is *Jesus' execution on the cross*, a punishment that *only the*

> *Roman authorities* could inflict and did frequently against rebels.
>
> —*Encyclopedia Britannica*, volume 10, page 148

Thus, yet again, the Crucifixion is viewed as a historical fact.

When the Jewish prophets, hundreds of years before Jesus was born, foretold that He would be crucified in Israel, the only means of inflicting capital punishment by the Jews was *by stoning and not by crucifixion* (Leviticus 20:2). Even after the Crucifixion, stoning remained the only means of inflicting capital punishment by the Jews (Acts 7:58). Crucifixion was prohibited as "a punishment that only the Roman authorities could inflict." For the prophecies concerning the Crucifixion to be fulfilled, a country such as Rome that utilized crucifixion had to conquer Israel. Awesome indeed!

> The *undeniable fact* that He was *crucified* by the *Romans* as a political Messianic pretender . . .
>
> —*Encyclopedia Britannica*, volume 10, page 148

> The period within which *His ministry and death occurred* may, however, be narrowed down with considerable accuracy on the basis of a synchronistic dating of the appearance of John the Baptist in the 15th year of Tiberius . . . which is confirmed by non-biblical sources.
>
> —*Encyclopedia Britannica*, volume 10, page 148

> The best clue for a reconstruction of the outward course of Jesus' passion is *given by His Crucifixion*. It proves that He was condemned and executed under Roman law as a *political rebel*.
> All reports agree that He died on a *Friday*.
>
> —*Encyclopedia Britannica*, volume 10, page 153

> But the phenomenon of the *whole Gospel tradition*, rightly understood, is an expression of the *faith*

> in the living Christ without which *neither a single word* or *deed* of Jesus nor His *passion* would have been handed down at all. The New Testament tradition *does not aim at preserving* the memory of Jesus as a figure of the past and telling only who Jesus was, but it wants to *proclaim who Jesus is*.
>
> —*Encyclopedia Britannica*, volume 10, page 154, under "The Story of Jesus and Faith in Jesus"

Thus, the *Encyclopedia Britannica* concludes that wherever there were witnesses or documents, they all were united in their conclusions that Jesus was crucified and rose from the dead.

Description of a Crucifixion

Encyclopedia Britannica, volume 3, page 266 describes *a* crucifixion:

> There were various methods of performing the execution. Usually, the condemned man, after being *whipped, dragged the crossbeam* of his cross to the place of punishment, where the *upright shaft* was already fixed in the ground. There he was stripped of his clothing and bound fast with *outstretched* arms to the *crossbeam* or nailed firmly to it through the *wrists*. The crossbeam was then raised high against the upright shaft and made fast to it about nine to twelve feet (approximately three meters) from the ground. Next, the *feet were tightly bound or nailed* to the upright shaft. A *ledge* inserted about halfway up the upright shaft gave some support to the body; evidence for a similar ledge for the feet is rare and late. Over the *criminal's head* was placed a *notice* stating the *name and his crime*. Death, apparently caused by *exhaustion* or by *heart failure*, could be *hastened by shattering the legs* with an iron club, but the medical reasons for death are not fully understood.

> Crucifixion was most frequently used for *political or religious agitators*, pirates, slaves, or those who had no civil rights. In 519 B.C., Darius I, king of Persia, had 3,000 political opponents crucified in Babylon; in 88 B.C., Alexander Jannaeus, the Judaean king and high priest, had 800 Pharisaic opponents crucified; in 71 B.C., Marcus Crassus, the Roman triumvir, ordered the crucifixion of 6,000 rebellious slaves; and in about A.D. 32, Pontius Pilate had Jesus of Nazareth put to death by crucifixion.

The above account is not based upon biblical studies but on *secular* studies. This account of *a* crucifixion in the *Encyclopedia Britannica* is totally consistent with the account of *the* crucifixion of Jesus in the New Testament as follows:

1. *Jesus and Simon* each carried the cross and thus "*dragged the crossbeam* of the cross" (John 17:17 and Mark 15:21).
2. Jesus "was *stripped* of His clothing and *bound* fast with outstretched arms to the crossbeam" (Mark 15:24 and Matthew 27:35).
3. Jesus was "*nailed* firmly to it through the wrists."
4. "Over the criminal's head was *placed a notice* stating his name and his crime"—this was placed by Pontius Pilate (John 19:19).
5. Death was caused "*by heart failure*," as will be discussed later.
6. Jesus' death was not "hastened by shattering the legs with an iron club" because when the soldier came to shatter His legs, he found that He was already dead (John 19:32-33).
7. Jesus was a "*religious agitator*" for which crucifixion was frequently used.

Crucifixion Was Not Heard Of When These Prophecies Were Written

How profoundly and convincingly persuasive that King David and Isaiah, 500 and 250 years, respectively, before crucifixion was even on the historical scene, prophesied that the Messiah would meet His death by this then unknown means of crucifixion. Crucifixion was first inflicted in 519 B.C., (*Encyclopedia Britannica*, volume 3, page 266). Thus, when David and Isaiah were given their revelations about the crucifixion of Jesus, *crucifixion was not even on the historical scene*.

Pathology Confirms Jesus Died by Heart Failure

The conclusion that Jesus' death was caused by "heart failure" was unknowingly verified *by John* at the foot of the Cross of Jesus:

> The soldiers therefore came, and broke the legs of the first man, and of the other man who was crucified with him; but coming to Jesus, when they saw that He was already dead, they did not break His legs; *but one of the soldiers pierced His side with a spear, and immediately there came out blood and water.*
>
> —John 19:32-34

This account was not by a Jewish pathologist but a Jewish *fisherman*. Is John's observation of blood followed by water from Jesus' side physiologically sound? Is such to be expected after a person is crucified?

Experiments and studies have concluded that crucifixion results in death either by a *ruptured heart* or suffocation. The observation by John of blood, followed by water, establishes as we will see that Jesus' death was by a ruptured heart. Josh McDowell in his book *The Resurrection Factor*, quotes Dr. C. Truman Davis on page 48 as follows:

> Davis relates that there was "an escape of watery fluid from the sac surrounding the heart. We, therefore, have rather conclusive postmortem evidence that Christ died not from the usual crucifixion of the heart by fluid in the pericardium."

McDowell, in another book, *Evidence That Demands a Verdict*, writes on pages 198 and 199 regarding the conclusions of Dr. Samuel Houghton, a physiologist from the University of Dublin. Dr. Houghton said that the crucifixion and death of Jesus was caused by a combination of blood in the lungs and rupture of the heart. This diagnosis was confirmed when the side of Jesus was pierced, which released blood followed by water. Dr. Houghton concludes, "There remains, therefore, no supposition possible to explain the recorded phenomenon except the combination of the crucifixion and *rupture of the heart*."

The "fluid in the pericardium" looks like water, which explains physiologically what John observed at the foot of the cross of Jesus that "there came out blood and water."

King David, a thousand years before the crucifixion of Jesus, poetically foretold what Dr. Davis and Dr. Houghton described as fluid in the pericardium, which would have looked like water, when he wrote that His heart would be like *wax* and it would *melt* within Him:

> I am poured out like *water* . . . my heart is like *wax*, it is *melted* within me.
>
> —Psalm 22:14

Other Secular Historians Confirm the Historical Fact of the Crucifixion

Many other non-biblical and non-Christian sources refer to the crucifixion and resurrection of Jesus. Jewish historian Flavius Josephus, writing at the end of the first century A.D., wrote in *Antiquities* 18.3.3:

> Now there was about this time Jesus, a wise man, if it be lawful to call Him a man; for He was a doer of wonderful works, a teacher of such men as receive the truth with pleasure. He drew to Him many Jews, and also many of the Greeks. This man was the Christ. And when Pilate had condemned

> Him to the cross, upon His impeachment by the principal man among us, those who had loved Him from the first did not forsake Him, for He appeared to them alive on the third day, the divine prophets having spoken these and thousands of other wonderful things about Him. And even now, the race of Christians, so named from Him, had not died out.

Again, Josephus states in *Antiquities* 20.9.1:

> After the death of the procurator Festus, when Albinus was about to succeed him, the high priest Ananius considered it a favorable opportunity to assemble the Sanhedrin. He therefore caused *James the brother of Jesus*, who was called *Christ*, and several others, to appear before this hastily assembled council, and pronounced upon them the sentence of *death by stoning*. All the wise men and strict observers of the law who were at Jerusalem expressed their disapprobation of this act . . . Some even went to Albinus himself, who had departed to Alexandria, to bring this breach of the law under his observation, and to inform him that Ananius had acted illegally in assembling the Sanhedrin without the Roman authority.

The *Search for the Messiah* by Eastman and Smith states this regarding Roman historian, Tacitus:

> Cornelius Tacitus, born circa 52-55 C.E., became a senator in the Roman government under Emperor Vespasian. He was eventually promoted to governor of Asia. Writing in the year 116 C.E., in his annals, he writes of the burning of Rome in 64 C.E. and how Caesar Nero had tried to stop the rumor that he [Nero] was behind the destruction.

> Therefore, to scotch the rumor (that Nero had burned Rome), Nero substituted as culprits, and punished with the utmost refinements of cruelty, a class of men, loathed for their vices, whom the crowd *styled Christians*. *Christus*, the founder of the name, had undergone the *death penalty* in the reign of Tiberius, by sentence of the procurator *Pontius Pilatus*, and the pernicious superstition was checked for a moment, only to break out once more, not merely in Judea, the home of the disease, but in the capital itself, where all things horrible or shameful in the world collect and find a vogue . . .
>
> They *(the Christians)* were covered with wild beasts' skins and torn to death by dogs; or they were *fastened on crosses*, and, when daylight failed were burned to serve as lamps by night. Nero had offered his Gardens for the spectacle, and gave an exhibition in his Circus, mixing with crowd in the habit of a charioteer, or mounted on his car. Hence, in spite of a guilt which had earned the most exemplary punishment, there arose a sentiment of pity, due to the impression that they were being sacrificed not for the welfare of the state but to the ferocity of a single man.

Lucan of Samosata, a Greek satirist, wrote a remarkable statement regarding the Church in 170 C.E.:

> The *Christians*, you know, worship a man to this day—the distinguished personage who introduced their novel rites, and *was crucified* on that account. You see, these misguided creatures start with the general conviction that they are *immortal* for all time, which explains the contempt of death and voluntary self-devotion which are so common among them; and then it was impressed on them by their original lawgiver that they are *all brothers*,

> from the moment that they are converted, and deny the gods of Greece, and worship the *crucified sage*, and live after his laws. All this they take quite on *faith*, with the result that they despise all worldly goods alike, regarding them merely as common property.

Secular sources, in addition to the *Encyclopedia Britannica*, Cornelius Tacitus, Lucan, and Josephus that refer to the crucifixion and resurrection of Jesus, are the Roman historians Seutonius, Plinius Secundus and Justin Martyr; Samaritan Thallius; Syrian Mara Bar-Serapion; and as above indicated, the Jewish Talmud.

How important is our belief that Jesus rose from the dead? Eternity is determined by our answer:

> If you confess with your mouth Jesus is Lord... you will be saved.
>
> —Romans 10:9

The Trial of Jesus Was by Oppression

Isaiah prophesied that the arrest and trial of Jesus would be accomplished "by oppression"(Isaiah 53:8). The Mishnahic law was violated, and this prophecy fulfilled when the following Mishnahic laws were violated and His death thereby accomplished by oppression:

1. Criminal proceedings *could not occur after sunset*, but they did.
2. No arrest could be consummated by religious authorities obtained through a bribe, but it was through Judas.
3. Judges of the Sanhedrin were not allowed to *participate in the arrest*, but they did in the Garden of Gethsemane.
4. No trials could be held *before the morning sacrifice*, but they were.
5. *Two or three witnesses* were required for a conviction, and those witnesses had to *agree* in their testimony, but they did not.
6. Procedurally, the *defense first presented* their evidence and thereafter the prosecution, but no defense was even allowed.
7. The accused was not allowed to testify against *himself*, but Jesus did.
8. The person condemned to death could *not be scourged* or *beaten* beforehand, but Jesus was.

11. In capital punishment cases the trial and the verdict had to be *separated by twenty-four hours*, but it *was not*.

12. Charges could *not originate* with the *Sanhedrin*, but *they did*.

13. A *unanimous verdict* for guilt was *unlawful* because it would be impossible for all members of the Sanhedrin to agree without a *plot* being responsible for such a unanimous vote, but it was unanimous.

14. Judges were required to be *humane and kind*, but they were not.

15. The accused could not be condemned because *of* his own words, but Jesus was.

16. All trials must be conducted in the *Hall of Judgment* located in the temple compound, but they were not.

17. The verdict and sentence thereon had to be *separated by* three days, but they were not.

The Changed Lives of Those Close to Jesus After His Resurrection

Jesus predicted that His disciples, who had been with Him during His entire ministry and had witnessed His miracles, would scatter, go to their homes, and leave Him alone after his arrest (John 16:32). The Bible records this happening upon Jesus being arrested in the Garden of Gethsemane, when His disciples "left Him and fled" (Matthew 26:56). As a trial lawyer, I am wary of a witness or client who never admits doing anything wrong. On the other hand, it has been my experience that those witnesses or clients who forthrightly admit mistakes in their lives are usually telling the truth in other aspects of their testimony.

The Bible is full of admissions by the authors that they were sinners and made tragic mistakes. A more stark example cannot be posed than when Matthew admitted that when Jesus was arrested in the Garden of Gethsemane, he and the other disciples became cowards and "left Him and fled." After the Crucifixion, they returned to the Upper Room, where they were found by

Jesus cowering with the doors shut for fear that the Jews would come after them (John 20:19). After His Resurrection, the disciples were changed from cowards to men willing to sacrifice their lives for Jesus. History records that all the apostles died a *martyr's death* for their belief in the resurrected Lord except John, who died on the island of Patmos, where he was banished for his beliefs. The only event that occurred from the time they were cowards and when they became martyrs was when they observed the resurrected Jesus Christ.

The half-brothers of Jesus, despite observing His miracles, did not believe in Him (John 7:5). Jesus had four half-brothers and at least two half-sisters born to Mary after the birth of Jesus (Matthew 13:55-56). Joseph was the father of His half-brothers and half-sisters. After His half-brothers observed the resurrected Jesus, they too, believed in Him and accepted their half-brother Jesus as their Savior and Messiah. Judas (not Judas Iscariot, who betrayed Him), who wrote Jude, and James, two of His half-brothers (Mark 6:3 and Matthew 13:55), record this faith in the books written by them in the New Testament.

In the April 8, 1996 edition of *Newsweek*, an article called "Rethinking the Resurrection" attacked the historical accuracy of the crucifixion and resurrection of Christ. There was, however, a telling admission regarding the disciples:

> And yet, if the New Testament is to be believed, it was the appearance of the resurrected Christ that lit the flame of Christian faith, and the power of the Holy Spirit that fired a motley band of fearful disciples to proclaim the risen Jesus throughout the Greco-Roman world. According to the late German Marxist philosopher Ernst Bloch, "It wasn't the morality of the Sermon on the Mount which enabled Christianity to conquer Roman paganism, but the *belief* that Jesus had been *raised* from the dead . . . ."

The First Biblical Witnesses to Jesus' Resurrection Were Women

In Jewish society, the testimony of a woman carried very little weight. Yet, according to the Bible, the first witnesses to Jesus' resurrection were women. If this was a feigned account attempting to fool the reader that Jesus really rose from the dead, Jewish authors never would have selected women as their first witnesses to such resurrection.

The *Newsweek* article had this to say about that:

> What is significant here is that the first witnesses to the Risen Christ were women, not men. Had the story been invented solely for propaganda purposes, the early Christians would have made men the first witnesses, since the testimony of women carried far less authority in the patriarchal Jewish society.

If Jesus Was Stoned, He Was Not the Messiah

The Mishnah and the Talmud, written by Jewish authors after the Crucifixion, record that the Romans took away the power of capital punishment from the Jewish Sanhedrin exactly forty years before 70 A.D., which would be 30 A.D., the very year of Jesus' crucifixion. If Jewish law had been carried out and Jesus had been stoned rather than crucified, He would not have been the Messiah because the prophecies required that the Messiah be *crucified* (Psalm 22:16, Isaiah 53:5, and Zechariah 12:10). Again, profoundly and convincingly persuasive!

Jesus Said that Only He Could Fulfill the Prophecies Concerning the Crucifixion and Resurrection

Jesus explained to the "great multitude" arresting Him in the Garden of Gethsemane that the prophecies concerning His Crucifixion and Resurrection had to be fulfilled by Him when He asked the rhetorical question in Matthew 26:54: "How then shall the Scriptures be fulfilled, that it must happen this way?"

And again in Matthew 26:56: "But all this has taken place that the Scriptures of the prophets may be fulfilled."

How the Resurrection Date Changed the Calendar

In order to change the Julian calendar (B.C.) to the Gregorian calendar (A.D.), it was necessary to establish a starting point for the Gregorian calendar. The starting point used was the date of the Resurrection. *Encyclopedia Britannica* (volume 3, page 602) discusses how this date was determined:

> Easter being a festival of the Resurrection had to depend on the dating of the Crucifixion, which occurred three days earlier and just before the Jewish Passover.

In this one sentence, it is clear that the *fact* of the Resurrection was never in doubt, only its precise date.

In sum, there was never a debate as to whether the Resurrection occurred, only as to its precise *date*. To determine this starting point of the Gregorian calendar, reference was made to the gospels and other historical documents.

Conclusion: The Crucifixion and Resurrection Were Never Questioned by Any Historians, Documents, or Witnesses

It is irresistibly noteworthy that nowhere in this historical account of the trial, crucifixion, and resurrection of Jesus Christ, or in any "ancient documents," are any witnesses, documents, accounts that question *the historical fact* that Jesus Christ was crucified and the *historical fact* that He was resurrected from the dead. Therefore, I, as a trial lawyer, would have to advise my client, who asked me to prove the truth or the hoax of the trial, crucifixion, and resurrection of Jesus, that *all* witnesses and *all* documents and *all* historians reveal this Crucifixion and Resurrection to be the truth.

The next chapter, in one short paragraph, establishes that the Bible and its prophecies, as well as other ancient documents discussed in this book, are admissible into evidence. Thus, you the jury and reader will be able to determine if prophecies were made hundreds and even thousands of years before Christ and whether they were fulfilled.

The Bible, as Well As Many of the Other Documents Referred to in This Book, Would Be Admissible in Court as "Ancient Documents"

16

California Evidence Code Section 1331 would admit the Bible, as well as all other documents referred to in this book, as "ancient documents." This law provides:

> Evidence of a statement is not made in admissible by the hearsay rule if the statement is contained in a writing *more than thirty years old* and the statement has been since generally *acted upon as true* by persons having an interest in the matter.

The final chapter is the verdict that you, as the jury, will undoubtedly render based on the evidence set forth in this book.

The Verdict

17

Based upon the evidence in this book, the reader's verdict should be:

The Bible is undeniably the inspired Word of God, authored by God the Father and the Holy Spirit, because no book could be written prophesying with such precise accuracy unless by divine inspiration.

The Messiah and Son of God, described in the New Testament, is the same Messiah and Son of God described in the Hebrew Scriptures.

God the Father, God the Son and God, the Holy Spirit described in the Hebrew Scriptures is the one and only God who is similarly identified in the New Testament.

And finally, because the facts of the Bible are true, it would be foolish to reject its theology, which is that the only way to God the Father is through His Son, Jesus Christ (John 14:6).

My Comments Regarding This Verdict

The evidence is clear. What one does with this evidence is the most important question any person can or will be confronted with. *Eternity* is in that answer.

The most personally persuasive evidence that I have that

Jesus Christ is the Son of God is because He lives within me. Every day as a believer in Christ is more thrilling than the day before. Christ has proven Himself to be all-sufficient for me under all conditions. He has added a dimension to my life that is awesome and all-pervasive.

Why was I looking for a loophole when I initiated my three-month study back in 1976? Why was I frightened as to where this study would lead? My concern was giving up a lifestyle and things that I interpreted as being meaningful. Upon accepting Christ, however, I discovered that the things I gave up were meaningless and rubbish. Christ teaches us that this life is to be embraced with thankfulness and enjoyed (1 Corinthians 6:12 and 10:23). So, I gave up nothing and gained everything.

During my research and writing this book, I became more awed, amazed, and convinced that Jesus Christ is the true God. The thrill of this truth becomes more and more undeniable.

This book was written so you would become a believer in the King of Truth, Jesus. The Bible warns about the consequences of unbelief in Revelation 20:15:

> And if anyone's name was not found written in the book of life, he was thrown into the lake of fire.

The Bible also warns to handle "accurately the word of truth" in 2 Timothy 2:15:

> Be diligent to present yourself approved to God as a workman who does not need to be ashamed, handling accurately the word of truth.

Jesus Explained in John 8:32 that *the Truth Shall Set You Free . . .*

You are probably wondering—free from what? Based upon my personal experience, it has meant:

- Free from the confusion of what is the truth.
- Free from the confusion that Jesus is really the Messiah and

Son of God.

• Free from the confusion as to the meaning of life.

• Free from the confusion whether there is life after death and where I will spend it.

• Free from the confusion of how I can make a difference here on earth.

> But the fruit of the spirit is love, joy, peace, patience, kindness, goodness, faithfulness, gentleness, self-control.
>
> —Galatians 5:22-23

What can one do to be assured of everlasting salvation and also peace on this earth? Romans 10:9 provides that answer:

1. *Confess with your mouth your belief* that Jesus is Lord;
2. *Believe in your heart* that *God raised Him* from the dead;
3. And you will be *saved*.

This need not be said in a cathedral but, rather, at any place and any time.

So, do we have a verdict?

Or is the jury still out with you?

Scripture Index

For Making This Book Possible

I would like to thank Higgins Bailey, my pastor Kevin Springer, Mike Smith, and Dave Fulton. Mike Yorkey, who did a fine job editing the book, was indispensable in helping me get this book published. And a special thanks to Milt McKenzie for his encouragement and financing this project.